THE HEALING-LADDER EXPERIENCE

PAT PAULST

WESTBOW
P R E S S®
A DIVISION OF THOMAS NELSON
& ZONDERVAN

WestBow Press books may be ordered through booksellers or by contacting:

WestBow Press
A Division of Thomas Nelson & Zondervan
1663 Liberty Drive
Bloomington, IN 47403
www.westbowpress.com
844-714-3454

ISBN: 978-1-6642-3273-0 (sc)
ISBN: 978-1-6642-3274-7 (hc)
ISBN: 978-1-6642-3275-4 (e)

Library of Congress Control Number: 2021911680

Print information available on the last page.

WestBow Press rev. date: 06/09/2021

CONTENTS

INTRODUCTION

Thirty-six years ago, I began my healing process that changed my life completely. The process has involved the support of wonderful caring friends with the ability to ask me the right questions at critical times, counseling, graduate school, and a considerable amount of time in private, personal searching. Consequently, I have discovered tools helpful for me to reach self-described goals in addition to learning a lot about myself. In the earliest stages, the healing process was all-consuming and I experienced both physical and psychological pain on a regular basis in the first months.

However, as time passed allowing me opportunities to identify and celebrate various accomplishments I had made, the work I assigned myself began to feel less threatening and less difficult as the big picture of my life story started to become clear. I believe, if I had identified the concepts presented in the pages of this book years earlier, it would not have taken as long to arrive at the place I am today. My goals are not the same as the ones written twenty-five years ago as I now experience living in the Light. Today, I am consciously aware of positivity in my environment without listing it as a self-defined goal I am striving to accomplish. I also spend much more time in my life today looking forward with anticipation instead of backward with anxiety.

Although negative situations arise periodically interrupting my plans for a given day, it is usually an automatic reaction to pull from the following concepts and tools I identify as appropriate in examining connections between current and past situations to help me make healthy decisions today. I have found that if I do not take time for a deep breath allowing me to immediately turn to these concepts, I tend to have a difficult day or two.

Although my life story is not your life story, my desire is that you will find something here you feel will be productive for you to use also. The only page current in each of our stories is the one we are writing today. The rest of our life story is in the past and future. Consequently, can we agree that in this day, we are at a pivotal point between our past and our future? This thought alone may help you in deciding how or what context in the following pages may be of benefit for you to experience positivity in your future life-story chapters.

Some of my pages can be grouped together forming layers; some involving years. Examining a layer instead of a single situation, speeds my overall healing process. Although all of us have probably already lost all control over past pages in our life story; there may be situations or, possibly layers, in the past that are still creating negativity in our lives today because we have not recognized them (or, perhaps, are just trying desperately to pretend they do not exist). Consequently, we may be walking around in an undefined daze making unidentified choices that do not lead to the positive we prefer for today.

Because I cannot change past experiences that started me on my conscious healing journey, I have reached the conclusion that what I need to fix is the effect I allow the past to have on my today. If one accepts such an idea as truth, the page currently being written in a life -story has the potential of bringing a smile next year at this time. I am thankful I am currently in a place that allows me to define such a goal. Hopefully, these pages will allow you to define personal goals and tools to help you be able to say that you wish the rest of the pages in your life story will be much like the one you are experiencing in this day.

Conversations with others familiar with the following information have caused me to recognize that not only victims struggle; but also, those wishing to help. Because my healing-ladder experience taught me my life-story pages includes self-definitions of victim/survivor/helper, I have added chapter addendums to further examine my journey as self-defined believer. Although I was raised in a church and became a believer as a child, upon high-school graduation I consciously chose to turn away from anything and everything 'religious' in search of a totally different life than I had so far experienced. For twenty-nine years I lived the result of that choice until a life experience "threw me into a pit" causing me to define self as a broken, totally helpless victim.

The chapter addendums are written to offer specific information regarding my experiences and conclusions about what I believe and how I wish to define my goals in the last chapters of my story which have end up defined as <u>totally different</u> from those prior to the pit experience; except for a desire to help others. I believe the tools and approaches in the addendums will not only help, but also enable anyone to define them as useful in attaining positive goals.

EXAMINING TOOLS

I define a tool as an aid that I can use or an action I am able to take to help me prevent negativity today involving a past situation. Once I have labeled an unacceptable effect of the past situation and identified a possible end goal as well as the first step required to reach the goal; the tool I choose will allow me to begin to work on the first step. But, I realize, your first step may be different than mine. Your goals will not be the same as mine, because you and I could be in the same room at the same time and experience it individually causing that specific situation to read differently in our life stories. We may even prefer different approaches in our examination of the past situation we shared.

SUPPLEMENT to EXAMINING TOOLS

1. If you often sense negativity in your days and cannot identify it; hang in there! As you begin to remember situations and start using the tools, you will be surprised at the number of answers you will find. It is frustrating trying to fix something which has not yet been identified. Take a deep breath right now, maybe four would be a better choice.

2. You may have already made an identification, perhaps connected to the choosing of this book, as something you would like to be changed at some future date. If so, you may decide to write it now as a goal. I suggest no more than two, as you may make changes and probably add others. I also like to date everything allowing me to recognize the changes in my life from one date to another.

3. Why not kick off your shoes, go to your favorite chair; or simply smile for making this choice today. Celebrations are so important at each step in the healing process so giving yourself a pat on the back as a quick celebration is great! Somehow, a quick celebration helps one acknowledge a step has been taken to aid in today's page in one's life story to be more positive.

4. In the next section, I suggest a 'who-done-it' television show to help you. Perhaps you would like to watch one, if time allows, before you continue. You could label the activity as a reward if you enjoy 'who-done-it' television shows.

TOOLS ADDENDUM

I looked up the word 'abuse' in a student dictionary I reference often currently and in past years before typing this page. Adults are not the only people dealing with abuse in their lives. I have been involved in conversations with first graders identifying self as abuse victims. And they were smart enough to use that dictionary to try to get answers. I have discovered it is not only interesting but also helpful to 'look up' definitions of words that I and others are using in conversations. It is important for me, when in a helper role, to ask the other for personal identifications of words he/she is using in a conversation as our personal meanings of a word we are both using may vary. I now believe that who I am, as defined by others as well as by me, in a current day is impacted by my personal life-story pages experienced by me alone and not the 'others'. Not only do I believe these applications apply to me in any given day; but also, to the 'others'.

Years ago, in response to a college-class assignment, I defined the results of abuse as defining one or self as a 'non-entity'. Perhaps another way to say it is: "I was, or am, being treated as though I am a dog". I prefer the first definition, perhaps because I have a dog at this moment sleeping on a chair across from me wrapped in a blanket. If my definition involves more than myself, the healing process can be complicated as well as difficult. Consequently, it may be a requirement at this early stage to think about my capabilities, responsibilities, and choices. Who is responsible for me? What/who am I capable of changing? Am I possibly making choices that are unhealthy for me? Could I possibly make choices to use tools or behave in a manner that will not only extend the healing time for me; but, possibly, also hurt others?

The most important tool I use today when sitting with my life-story book open, is my accessibility to an all-knowing God. If someone is sitting with me who defines self as broken or needing help, I try to always remember to turn to God as my first step. It is

God who has the clear picture, neither one of us. So, in the role of helper, I also ask God to guide me. I passionately believe that it is always important to remember I am not the one who lives the life of another. I know what it feels like to have someone commenting on my life-story who was not present; making assumptions as to what work I have or have not accomplished in my life. I now will ask others in conversations I experience to define words they are using only to discover they struggle in doing so. Consequently, as a helper, I have a goal to only use terms I can readily define. I have experienced individuals, including some within church families, who respond to something I say with: "Well, you need to _____ In response to a scenario I have shared from my life without questioning any insight I, myself, may have about me. I define that as judging. I am the one who lived each chapter of my life story; no other human. If another is sharing and I am listening, that person is the only human present who has lived his/her life-story pages. I wish each believer with whom I come into contact would believe the same. It is a tremendous help and encouraging to me when I turn to someone in the church body for support today who agrees; and, more so when I was in the pit. My personal first choice for human help when I am hurting, is a fellow believer. A helper is not an easy role to take when you care and want to help another, however.

If you are in the pit and cannot yet stand; I know that God is aware and is willing to help you gain the insight and strength to stand as He did for me. If you are a helper, you probably will never hear the whole story. If I am trying to help an adult who has trouble crawling; I hope I would not say, 'you need to stand and walk'. It is also possible you may not know what this individual has accomplished or not yet tackled in his/her healing experience. When I first started on the healing ladder, I could not have stood without hanging on to something...not the time for somebody to remind me that I was required to do what I defined as impossible. Bringing up 'what I need to do' may have knocked me off the ladder as I was struggling just to hang on. These were just the first steps of my healing process. Please give an individual a break, who has just decided to try and figure things out to have the life they desire ... and listen.

When beginning the healing process, one may easily be operating under the teaching of abuse, defining self as worthless and weak; I certainly was. I also was not certain that I would be able to hang onto the ladder, not to mention having the strength for anything more. Which sounds like a good place to start the healing process before dealing with anything more! Driving back one night from my first experience with counseling sessions, I have a clear memory from what ended up being my last session with the person. I considered crossing the center line of a highway to drive under an oncoming truck to end it all resulting from a comment made by the helper in the session I accepted as indicating an issue was my fault. As a helper, please keep in mind that one is required to stand to wear the complete armor God provides. You may not be correctly labeling the abilities currently available to the person to whom you are speaking. And, if you are reading this hoping to find help for you to heal; please recognize that I am now typing this page desiring to give you something to help you get where I am today. I was ready on that highway driving home that night to end it all questioning if I could ever become anything 'worth spitting on'. I cannot identify with each chapter in your book; I have not lived your life. Just as I cannot expect others to identify with my story. However, I trust that each of us has the right to expect respect from others. Please try and remember as you pick and choose tools to use that: as a believer, you **DO** have an Ally who has been with you, has every answer you require, and knows you better than anyone else ... including you. You **CAN** do this; I know because I have. I never experienced considering suicide again. **And** God will be with you on each step of this journey. You will gain the inner strength to follow Him if you make the choice to do it. In fact, you may agree with me when this healing journey ends …. totally amazed at the differences in your definitions of self. And guess what…it keeps getting even better over the years with God's help. Why not start picking and choosing what fits for you.

One description I have heard used in the healing process is a sense of being in a war. If you have sensed that you are on some type of a battlefield, I have some encouraging news for you! There is a tool available to believers that I still use regularly and will be referencing within the addendums. Early in my healing process, I was the person I tend to be when leaning into anger. Had I chosen to turn to God for guidance then, instead of questioning and/or ignoring Him, my healing-ladder experience would probably have been shortened by years! I think any believer who chooses to heal from abuse is going to be involved in spiritual warfare. And I also think that the believers, choosing to assist the 'victim', are also involved in spiritual warfare. Consequently, I will frequently be referencing the warfare and what the Bible states believers have been provided to face it. Some background in this warfare might be helpful for you.

The Bible talks about Jesus Christ living on earth as 100% man. He was born, lived until adulthood, then suffered and died covered in sins of all humanity (He was the only man who never sinned). Jesus Christ chose to do that for anyone who chooses to believe in Him thus allowing believers to spend eternity with Him.

Here is the part about the 100% man I want to zero in on: Abuse 'victims' are broken. Because Jesus Christ was 100% man, He 'gets' us! How cool is that? I always hope I remind a fellow believer of that who is sitting with me defining self a 'broken victim'. When I was broken in the pit screaming at Jesus, He was with me. Years later, when praying for insight to help others but refusing to read a helpful book beside me on my nightstand because it was written by a Christian author, Jesus was with me patiently waiting for me to choose to follow His lead. I was angry and defining the paths I labeled as the wisest choices for what I wanted in my life.

He clearly understood the lessons on pages of my life story that I had not even yet recognized. Not only was Jesus by my side, He understood me having experienced the pain we suffer on earth... as He did also. He went to Heaven with physical scars from abuse on earth by humans. He 'gets' it and was silently with me when I was broken. When I chose not to turn to Him, but rather to fight leaning into my anger slipping and sliding in the pit; He was there, silently waiting. The idea of that alone is comforting to me. He waited patiently for me for years to turn to Him. I am saying this to you hoping it will help you in using the 'free will' that God gifts us wisely. And, I believe I have also been involved in spiritual warfare since the moment I turned to Him to follow His lead.

Verses in the Bible talk about when Jesus was not only abused by humans in various ways, but also tempted by Satan. The following is my theory regarding how I am affected by these stories: The devil and Jesus do not get along; but are enemies. So, all those years I was trying to survive on earth avoiding God as much as possible, I was pleasing the devil. However, when I began turning to God in the healing process, it threatened the devil. That is when the spiritual warfare enters the picture, I think. But the cool thing is this: Jesus has it covered. It is called "the armor of God" and is available to us as a gift from God. I think that, because we are humans and not God, we are no match for the devil; however, when Jesus was walking on earth waiting for the time to die for us to be with Him in Heaven and was tempted by Satan, the devil was the one that turned and ran! Instead of telling us to fight the devil in the war, the Bible teaches that God is our Ally and is with his followers on the battlefield fighting for us.

The armor will be discussed throughout the addendums. Just know that, as a believer, you have Someone right there with you helping you to stand in the full armor of God. You will be able to face the devil, and face him without fear; I know, because today...I can! You will also feel the strength and recognize the ability to accomplish what you define today as impossible following God's leading. Personally? I will take living in this day, any day. I can smile easily recognizing how I define my life today in comparison to before and during my time in the slime of the pit.

Truth must be important to God as it is described in the Bible as a piece of the armor of God. The Bible describes truth as a belt holding up the armor. And I learned that it is also telling me that, if I use my free will to study the Bible, I will not only learn the truth, but the truth sets me free. And guess what...God does not lie!

When I personally studied this information regarding the armor of God and was easily defining myself as being on some type of battlefield struggling to even stand, I started to use the information I was gaining and applying it to my healing process. I began to study my personal beliefs determining if I was 'living' what I said I 'believed'.

As believers, how often do we examine our definition of the 'truth' we are choosing to believe and follow? I believe it is of value to do so when in a healing process. I think it would be extremely helpful for one starting on the journey of healing to check whose definition he/she is using for a description of self. It took me a while after I was <u>off</u> the healing ladder to realize one of my biggest hurdles was my continuous accepting of how significant other humans in my life defined me. Perhaps it would be helpful continuing on this healing journey to choose to consider what God said to His followers about how <u>He</u> defines us and what He gifts us. When I feel I am on the battlefield, I find it helps me with this issue to ask myself the following questions regarding how I am defining me in the present day: Are the choices I am making now indicating I am a 'Child of God'? ... Do my actions reflect a belief that He loves me and does so with an everlasting love? … He is here with me. … He will support me in my times of need ... He will supply the required strength.

Do you believe the Lord only speaks truth? Do you believe you have been given free will to choose who you are going to follow and what you are going to believe in this healing journey? If so, can you agree that how one defines 'truth' could be important in climbing the healing ladder? If you believe God speaks the truth and knows all and loves us, then why not consider partnering with Him on the climb and turning to Him for insight?

EXAMINING APPROACHES

You may have identified a past situation you label as possibly being unresolved. Now, you want to determine how to correctly define what you need to do by examining the situation as you remember it.

If this were my assignment, it would be difficult for me to easily picture the scene in my mind. But, perhaps, that is exactly what you would likely do readily. If so, let your mind wander around the past setting observing the players and their actions as you would a 'who-done-it' show on television. This approach may be useful in your gaining valuable insight into the situation you have recalled. For instance, in concentrating on a past situation, I have remembered the look on the face of a significant other which has been helpful to me in understanding something I had missed before.

Perhaps you are a great listener; maybe you prefer books in which the characters are doing a lot of talking, rather than a book describing the environment as the person in the preceding paragraph would probably prefer. Or do you prefer listening to a book? It may be helpful if you also try to remember what the people are saying in your past situation. Perhaps their tone of voice would help you to gain insight. Watching a 'who-done-it', do you pay attention when a character's voice is shaky or hesitant? If so, try using this tool when thinking back to your past situation for answers.

Or, maybe, you are like I am and prefer to concentrate more on what significant others might have been feeling in the past circumstance. I am only successful in accomplishing this effectively when I do <u>not</u> look at self, but only the other. It has helped me to try to realize what a person is feeling as I remember their words and actions; however, I find I am only able to use this tool when I know a lot about the other person's life story. Trying to identify the emotions he/she experienced in a situation we shared has sometimes helped me understand the individual's behavior.

Using the above approaches while studying the whole picture each time a past situation came to mind often helped me recognize and dissolve much of the anger I had been harboring over the years regarding the incident. For example, would it surprise you that I discovered, in simply trying to identify the perspective of others who shared an experience with me, that they probably saw the picture much differently than I?

I decided their perception may be different than mine because their life story is different than mine. If true, then they are also at a different place than I, probably currently as well as in the past situation. Gaining an understanding of another's possible views in and about a past situation, without discussing it with them or without judging them, is difficult but not impossible with practice. And I was surprised to realize doing so lessened the anger I felt about the past situation. Consequently, the absence of so much anger unconsciously was allowing me to like myself more. As more time passed, I became aware that I was able to identify positive crowding out the negative in my daily life.

Trying to put myself in their place with their life story, as I personally came to understand it, also has allowed me to recognize and give up claiming undeserved guilt I oftentimes realized I was carrying from a past situation. As a result, I could breathe much easier and climb to the next step on the ladder, after a celebration.

I must add, however, that praying was involved asking for help in gaining an understanding that I recognized I needed before I felt I had the strength to do what I deemed was required of me to make any necessary changes to take care of me as I continued the climb on my healing ladder.

SUPPLEMENT to EXAMINING APPROACHES

1. Try to describe anything you learned about yourself by watching the television show.

2. If possible, label a past situation you think may be connected to a negative in your life currently.

3. Can you identify one unacceptable emotion or reaction you experience today that you believe may be connected to the situation you chose? If so, write it here; but, if not, you will have more opportunities as you go forward.

4. If you could change the emotion or reaction listed above, how would you be able to tell it had changed to what you desire? If appropriate, write the answer here as a goal.

5. As you examine various situations you choose from your life-story pages in your healing process, try to use what you described in the first question as a tool; it may help speed the process along.

APPROACHES ADDENDUM

When using the approach discussed in this addendum, I was not only fascinated, but found it extremely helpful to use my personal 'style/system' as a tool. The three most common 'personal styles' are visual, auditory, and kinesthetic. I realized that, when driving to a questionable location, I always say: "It feels like I should turn here." Consequently, I defined myself as 'kinesthetic'. I found it became much easier and quicker to study scenarios on the past pages of my life story using my 'style' as a tool.

I also found it extremely useful in helping others, as it allows one to converse in 'the other's language'. Here are some examples of how you can use this tool as a helper in conversing within the same style as the other:

> "I'm beginning to see that...." "So, from your point of view, then ..." = visual

> "I don't like him to ring my bell" "Your internal dialogue tells you..." =auditory

> "I felt pinned against the wall when..." "So, you get uptight when..." =kinesthetic.

Staying within the verbiage of the other can sometimes be very helpful. In my opinion it is helpful in creating a safe environment for the one who is asking for help, reacting to a hurtful situation, or just beginning the healing process.

The portion of the Bible regarding the disciples struggling in the boat in a storm and Jesus approaching them walking on the water has been encouraging to me throughout my healing process. If you are striving to help yourself or others, know that I am very thankful that I was reading this when I needed the message that Jesus 'gets me'. He has the capacity to understand what I am thinking...to speak the language I speak… and to identify my feelings. When I was struggling to simply meet the requirements for a paycheck to pay bills, Jesus was aware just as He saw the men struggling to row the boat in the storm to stay afloat. (Mark6:47-48) *Later that night, the boat was in the middle of the lake, and he was alone on land. He saw the disciples straining at the oars, because the wind was against them. Shortly before dawn he went out to them, walking on the lake.*" (NIV p.1091). Hopefully, thinking about how Jesus saw those followers and walked on the water out to assist them, it will be easier to recognize that He will do the same for us today. The Disciples could not stand; and neither could I when climbing on the healing ladder. So, take some deep breaths and keep going. It was necessary for me to identify wounds requiring me to address before they could be healed allowing me to stand and use the gift of the armor of God against the devil.

I recognized Jesus got into the boat and did not judge the Disciples. It meant a lot to me that when I was climbing up the healing ladder, the friends to whom I was turning treated me with respect, following that example, with caring rather than judging. They did not use words like: "you should… need to… have to". (I question if Job would have been a shorter book of the Bible had his 'friends' done the same!) I have talked with fellow believers who may be broken; but it does not mean they have stopped believing. I do not read where Jesus indicates that regarding His disciples. There were times when I was telling God that He was not there; now, looking back at that time, I can identify clearly that He was there with me. (A minister with whom I was sharing my brokenness story in his office said: "Excuse me…I'm confused…you were talking to Someone telling Him you didn't believe He was there?") ......Think about it.

MAKE IT CONCRETE

For me, personally, it is important to try to make each step in the healing process concrete. For instance, to have the goal of 'Be Happy' is great; but, if five people give a definition of 'Be Happy', you will likely have five various definitions. Try to think and work concretely as you go through the healing process. What would a day look like if you were happy? Try to define your goals in a concrete positive manner. How can one readily accomplish, and then celebrate accomplishing something, one cannot define? How will you be able to say, "Yes, I accomplished that goal; now, I will work on this one", if it has not been clearly defined?

It is extremely important to know when you have accomplished a goal and to celebrate. For instance, if you require a car to be happy; but do not have the money to pay for it, you may have to put other goals in front of the goal of buying a car. For instance, a goal may be to start school, or change jobs, or write down every time you spend a cent for a month to see if you are wasting money. Such work may help you to make a concrete goal for today that defines if, how, or what you need to change to accomplish the step goals on the path to meet the end goal to be happy.

Make your ideas and goals concrete so you will know when to celebrate. Define and decide: Step # 1 to meet a particular goal is_____, and then take the appropriate first step.

SUPPLEMENT to MAKE IT CONCRETE

1. If you have labeled two life goals, write one to three points under each that prove the goals will have been realized. You may need to think about this a while...I did.

2. Look again at the situation you chose to use. Also, in thinking about your current recurring effects, why did you choose that situation? Are you able to yet define something about you that may be preventing this past situation from staying in the past and not interrupting this day? If so, consider if this is a good time to write a now goal explaining how it will be a done deal when the goal is accomplished.

3. If you have a now goal written connected to a specific identified issue within you that is not ok, can you list one action under it that you can take today to start to resolve this issue?

4. If you take a headache pill for a stomach problem, it probably will not help. You may not have enough information yet to write goals; that's ok. There are a few more concepts following which may help, so just keep going.

5. What are you going to do today to celebrate what you have accomplished; and do not allow yourself to say you have accomplished nothing, because I know you are thinking about things in a different way. I discovered that It is a good idea to Celebrate at each step!

MAKE-IT-CONCRETE ADDENDUM

When I was at this stage in the healing process, I could not easily stand, and yet was facing a huge battle. If that is how you are feeling right now, I have some extremely good news for you, fellow believer! I know, this is not an easy little walk on the beach; to me the armor of God caused me to think: If I cannot even stand up, how can I survive a battle with Satan? I'll just give up... STOP!!... Here is the GOOD NEWS: There is ONLY ONE PIECE OF ARMOR THAT IS USED FOR OFFENSE. IT IS CALLED THE SWORD OF THE SPIRIT. IT IS CONCRETE. YOU DO NOT PUT IT ON, JUST OPEN IT. JESUS USED IT WHEN SATAN WAS TEMPTING HIM AND YOU CAN USE IT TODAY LYING ON YOUR FLOOR...STANDING=NOT REQUIRED... BECAUSE IT IS THE <u>BIBLE</u>...THE <u>WORD OF GOD</u>. In the Bible book of Hebrews 4:12, the Bible is described: *"For the word of God is alive and active. Sharper than any double-edged sword..."* (NIV p.1303).

The other night I called a friend and asked how much time she had as I wanted to read to her; she said twenty minutes before dinner was ready. I did not have a chance to read because she was sharing with me what she was experiencing with God. I thoroughly enjoyed the 'conversation' as I didn't have to be with her to feel her excitement. She described picking up her Bible and asking God to take her to the right page. Every time she did that, she became encouraged and looking forward rather than back. I don't know if she ever had the dinner because I listened to her excitement for two hours.

The Bible appears to be 'alive' to me in re-experiencing that evening. I have experienced the same in praying for God to show me something and then, when I go to the Bible, I re-read a passage but see something there I did not see before. Perhaps you have had a like experience. I do not believe it is required for me to tell God when I am struggling as Jesus 'gets me' and the Holy Spirit is always with me. The Bible helps me to feel and believe in a 'concrete' manner.

When Jesus was on earth facing the devil tempting Him, He used the Bible as a sword in my view. And that is what I strive to do when struggling. When I accomplish that goal, I recognize a strength I had not felt before. Various Bible verses describe the Word as being a sharp sword, alive, and lasting. Interesting, I think, that encouragement was given to those being attacked.

In reading the Bible for personal encouragement in my healing process I found that it does not only address those being attacked, but also the attacker. It describes how, when walking on earth: *"Jesus said to His disciples: 'Things that cause people to stumble are bound to come but woe to anyone through whom they come. It would be better for them to be thrown into the sea with a millstone tied around their neck than to cause one of these little ones to stumble'.* (NIV Luke 17:1-2 p. 1136)

Wow! Talk about being concrete! I have heard this verse quoted various times but never 'explained'. I would like to take a moment here to think 'out loud' to you. When I go to a Bible class or listen to a sermon; I want to learn and understand what is being said. But nobody needs to 'explain' this to me! Jesus said it to His disciples. Did not Jesus direct His disciples to teach others? Do you agree abuse may have been an important issue in His mind? I define this as a specific gift to me personally and to all who have abusive scenarios on their life story pages. The Bible shows me in this way that we are important to God. In my opinion, the verses start general and move quickly to specific. Note the first verse: *"people to stumble"*; but then...*"woe to anyone"*, not those...anyONE-- apparently it does not matter who he/she is nor how many. Now, the second verse: ...*"better for them"* ... must be ALL the anyONES. My fellow believer if your private life-story pages identify you as a victim, notice how Jesus used the word 'one' at the close of the sentences: *"to cause one of these"*. I react to this 'one' to be important to Jesus. I read in graduate classes that it is not unusual for one in a group to be victimized; verified in many of my conversations. The <u>one</u> (that is specific...not a group, but an <u>individual</u> ... the ONE of these). I read *"these little ones"* as HIS definition of the group around Him as He is speaking. I choose to believe that Jesus is speaking very concretely here referencing stories that were happening in that day and obviously still happening. I, personally, am thankful that I can be encouraged in concretely seeing how Jesus feels about my past-story page as I read these verses.

I believe these verses tell me very specifically that the person today who is sharing their abusive past with me is defined by Jesus as an individual who has a unique definition as do you and as do I. And He loves us...each one...equally and deeply enough to be extremely specific and concrete about what WILL BE DONE to those who cause us to stumble. Although he specifically described each of us as <u>one</u>; the uniqueness of each of us is recognized in the word 'stumble' in my opinion. I choose to define this as Jesus cares about me as He does about you and will gift us both equally by punishing the abuser equally for _____inflicted...allowing you and me to fill in that blank only recognizing to me that yes, our stories are ours and ours alone; but every one of us have this gift from Him. Thus, providing us the choice to accept that HE is aware of each of our experiences in life including the ones causing each of us to 'stumble'.

Today, years after stepping off the ladder onto the Foundation, I can also add that I believe Jesus totally 'gets' you and me. If you are reading this today while you are on this rung; know this: When I was on this rung, I was not thinking about how God understood my inadequacies. I had turned my back on Him and had not yet recognized He was down in that pit with me patiently waiting. My opinion of these verses, however, is that they also gift me and, possibly you, with the verification that Jesus recognizes the effects of abusive situations. I believe any abuse teaches an identification of unworthy, unequal, and weak. I passionately believe if anyone recognizes the struggle of an abuse 'victim', it is Jesus Who <u>chose</u> to come to earth to 'get it'. I wonder if any of the 'little ones' referenced in these verses have put their hands in His scars in Heaven sitting around Him in the circle up there; what a beautiful picture. Hopefully looking at this now will help give you encouragement to keep working on this path reminding you of His love and desire for you to become the survivor with strength to use the ability He has gifted you to follow His path to accomplish what you are able to accomplish for Him. You can do it. Talk to Jesus…He is right beside you this very second. I didn't and it took me longer to be a survivor than it will you if you just talk to Him…allow yourself to take deep breaths right now and Breathe HIM in.

Satan is a well-known liar, deceiver, and controller according to multiple Biblical passages. God loves His believers and has provided us with armor which wins against Satan. It is a 'concrete' piece of armor. I can hold the Bible, I can open and read His Words in the Bible, or I can choose to put it on the shelf closed--- the only offensive weapon-piece of the armor--- and I can use it anytime and anyplace. Standing is not a requirement and simply quoting from the Words of God in the Book will cause the devil to turn.

I know that, when I was at this stage in my healing experience, I was conscious of the concrete physical results of the abuse in addition to the psychological. So, if this is an issue for you, fellow 'victim' know that you are definitely not alone! (And, in a helper role, I choose not to be the one to bring this into the conversation generally…in some cases, if a helper of mine brought it up, I would probably get up and walk out!) I want to say here and now to you that, as I climbed the ladder using the steps in these chapters, the physical sensations decreased as I defined negative effects and concretely worked on my goals. I do not recall being specifically conscious of exactly when or how. Perhaps the broadening of the understanding of the total pictures and definitions help. But I can describe a very recent experience to you. I know this much…I was totally shocked the moment I recognized what was happening with my body as soon as the situation was overtaking me that I defined at the time as a physical trigger of a past abusive scenario.

Generally, in my daily life, I will choose to take stairs to an elevator … even if I am with a group going to the same place! (Do you think such a choice might have something to do with past-story pages involve being tied up in the attic and closet as a child!). Anyway, I had an appointment in an office to which I've gone 16 floors up in the elevator alone numerous times and have always chosen to not climb those particular stairs! I realized that it was taking too long and that it didn't feel like I had moved...then it hit! I started pushing buttons like crazy, yelling and knocking on the door...By the time I was able to read directions by the buttons and made a call, I was screaming at whomever answered. (all I had to do was push the button of the floor on which I walked into the elevator and the door opened--apparently because I had not moved. The gal expecting me knew the elevators had been shut off but forgot to give me directions on the phone and I did not know I was getting a call because I was driving to her office!). I did not realize how I had been affected physically until I walked (sort of) into the office and stood at the counter with my elbows on the counter holding my head while I tried to take deep breaths. When I turned from the counter to leave, I was questioning how I was going to drive home. I was talking to God. But He had me covered...another gal in the area when I stepped out of the elevator who was heading to the same garage floor on the next elevator and recognized I was in trouble. Guess what! God knows how to drive!!! My dog is too small to reach the foot pedal and steering wheel at the same time...I had no problem getting home with my hands on the wheel and foot on the pedal. But, yes, when out of the car walking to accomplish next two things on list before home; I was extremely conscious of God next to me as I wobbled around a little.

Initially in my healing process I did not recognize HE 'gets me'; trust me--today, no problem...I will not listen to anyone who says God was not with me in that car the other day and I can guarantee you that HE 'gets me' and HE 'gets you'. I do not believe HE is judging you nor is HE judging me when we are struggling or broken. My response was...God, why? How am I to use this experience? I had that elevator experience after I thought this addendum was completed! I guess you are supposed to know about this to help you or to help you help others like me! Know this much, if you are reading this to help you: When I was on the floor years ago desperately trying to identify what to do because I could not physically stand and my past-life pages were flashing across my mind, I now recognize I was that weak little girl still tied up in the attic and closet. But, the other day in that elevator and in the car with my hands on the wheel driving home from that experience; I definitely did <u>not</u> define myself as victim, nor did I define the experience as victimizing. I kept asking God out loud to help me 'get it right'... 'what was I supposed to do with the experience'... I knew I needed HIS help to understand correctly.

Do you feel broken at this point? Could your anger be blocking you from being efficient in your healing process today? Looking back in my life-story pages, this was the description of me. Today, I would also state that, early in my healing process, I was still turning to significant others for answers and help. It was not helping me step up on the next ladder rung. Now, I believe it was also extremely painful to those I was questioning. When I was broken and could not stand, I could not see beyond me. The others on the pages were not, and still are not, me. They were, and still are, living their pages... not mine. Others on the same pages would probably not define the scenarios as I did then nor now. And they may not have the answers I desired. If you think it may be possible that this also describes you at this point, it may be beneficial for you to examine how you are trying to get your answers.

It took me a long time before I replaced other humans with the All-Knowing One who was patiently waiting for me to turn to Him. He has also decreased the anger as well as other emotions addressed in upcoming addendums. Today I admit I still do not have every question answered, but I now know from experience that I may gain a surprising insight in an unexpected manner; sometimes not even immediately identified! HIS timing is different than mine. I have also experienced that it is not unusual today to gain a sudden clarity that would have caused a negativity within me then; but does not have that impact today. I am guessing that what I have just said may sound impossible; but it is true...I often respond on this day with something like: Wow! that finally makes sense...thanks, God!

It has been years now since I did the work described in these chapters and I have experienced much of the information offered in these addendums. Know the same is available to you. If you are currently a victim...know He will help you become the survivor. Keep turning to Him and tweaking what is on these pages to fit your story and healing process as you define it with HIS leading and it will not take you as long as it has me. So, let's keep going...take a couple of deep breaths.

SELF-TALK

I believe a prerequisite in anyone accomplishing goals is a sense of self-worth. In my case, self-worth (believing that I am as worthy as you) presented a big hurdle with which I struggled in the first stages of my conscious healing process. I also recognized early on that the struggle ahead was going to take all the strength I could muster. I had to believe I was worth the effort. Everything about me seemed to be not good enough, but rather: bad, sick, stupid, and impossible. I questioned if I would ever again feel somewhat normal.

One tool I began using immediately, particularly in the car driving out of traffic or sitting in a line of traffic at a light, was self-talk. Sitting at the wheel (hopefully with no one seeing me; or, if they did, thinking I was singing to the radio), aloud I would state my whole name followed with phrases like: "is a deserving person"..."is worthy"..."is capable"..."can do____". The latter became beneficial in encouraging me as I worked on the steps that I had defined to reach my end goal. Looking back to this time, it is surprising to me how self-talk such as, "I am as important as____" (whoever I was recognizing as 'the other' to whom I gave control of my thoughts in the past), helped give me the current belief that I am worthy of the work I am trying to do. In my life story, I believe this was a necessity early on to allow me to meet any type of personal goal.

SUPPLEMENT to SELF-TALK

1. If you have identified a negative opinion of yourself (perhaps secretly?), this may be a good time to ask yourself if there is something involved that may be preventing your healing process from being as affective as you hope it will be.

2. If you have not identified anything, practice self-talk by using it to celebrate. I found this a positive tool while working in each chapter: Aloud, state your full name and praise yourself for reading the material and thinking about it. See, you are already changing!

3. If you have identified a false negative opinion you accept about yourself, could it become a positive true opinion? If so, the next time you are alone, state aloud an appropriate sentence for you, describing the opinion you would like to believe for yourself and try it. Use future tense if you wish by saying, "I, full name, will be_____." and try it over and over. I used my sentence frequently for a month or two and recognized I was beginning to think differently by using self-talk and many of the other tools described as we move along.

4. Can you make a positive statement aloud right now about yourself? I am proud of you! I do not think you will be on the healing ladder for as long a time as I was. I spent a lot of time trying to figure out what to do to help myself.

SELF-TALK ADDENDUM

As a believer, I say I believe the Bible, I sing songs about the love of Jesus, and I say I want to follow Him. If I have a day now when I feel I am struggling, I find it helps to stop and consider the following questions:

Am I blaming Him for the consequence I suffer because of a choice I made?

Am I on a path searching to gain from earthlings what He provides?

Am I asking Him to follow me doing what I want to do this day?

Am I living reflecting His definition of me today?

What will today's choices, as a believer, show on my life-story page?

When I am trying to help another, am I practicing what I say I believe by following God's direction?

I am still far from perfection; and recognize I will never get there while on earth. But He still is with me and loves me; perfection is not a requirement.

I believe that any type of abuse includes belittling. Consequently, it is probable that any 'victim' has or is struggling to define self as equal to others. And, possibly living a facade in public by acting as a character in a play not in agreement with his/her/ honest definition of self. I also believe any person who has dealt with abuse deals with anger, and oftentimes shame, possibly not yet identified or is currently repressed to keep the secret enabling him/her/ to be accepted by other humans.

If equality is an issue for you, then you may be defining yourself as a non- equal and weak. In reading Paul's letter to the church family in Corinth, I was encouraged to accept the possibility that God's definition of me might differ from the definition earthlings may readily apply (including myself). In 1Corinthians 1:26-30, I believe Paul is addressing the issue: "*Brothers and sisters, think of what you were when you were called. Not many of you were wise by human standards; not many were influential; not many were of noble birth.*" (NIV p1238). I think of this verse when I question if I am capable, smart enough, strong enough to accomplish the assignments I identify him giving to me. I believe this passage can be an encouragement saying to anyone who is struggling: Guess what, God may be calling on you to do a very important job. So, why not turn to Him and His Word to gain the strength to stand? It's great to have a group of friends who are nonjudgmental; but that's not always available. I do believe the Bible was written for all. My personal experience has taught me that it is not unusual to read the same passage at different times and react differently; others have said the same. The Bible is an exciting piece of the armor of God to use for many purposes.

I also found journaling often offered me a sense of relief and insight. By always dating what I wrote in a diary daily or journaling; I often had a reason to celebrate amazing growth when looking back at it. And a strange thing I did years ago, that I have sitting on a piece of furniture, is an unopened small unexpected present. My friend has no memory of giving it to me. The box is small, and I do not know what is in it; neither does my friend. Because, when I received it, I decided to save it to open if I ever again felt lonely and a victim. However, now I look at it and smile because I've probably had it twelve years; and yet have not felt the need to open it. My belief is that when I die, someone else will be questioning it (or me!). Each time I move it while dusting, or I happen to glance at it, I smile and say a prayer of thanks. It also gives me an opportunity for a moment of positive self-talk of successful hard work accomplished.

Although I may become discouraged today, I no longer define myself using the abusive definition. Neither do readily accept negative definitions of me offered by others within my environment. If I am praying regularly and have the goal of following His lead instead of mine, I feel an equal to those who may be judging me. So, let's keep reading and discovering some concrete steps for good health!

TRIGGERS

Today I still use self-talk when I identify a trigger, which I define as an effect I experience in the present connected to a past situation in my life story. Some triggers are to be expected and some are totally a surprise. All of us, I believe, experience triggers in our lives. For instance, a death of a loved one causes an expected affect every year for many because each year when the anniversary date of the death comes around, they will think about that person. A friend of mine has chosen to control such an anniversary by going to a favorite location where she and her husband had shared many fun times. She quietly sits while bringing to mind those happy memories. Thus, the concrete manner she has chosen to create a positive each year on a certain date has been an excellent example to me as to how one can create a positive today from a past negative.

In my view, advising another to forget about a negative trigger from the past may not be a positive piece of advice. I have recently read that when one 'stuffs' past negatives, the positives are also forgotten. I know this is true because it has been my personal experience. Healing from abuse is not a warm, fuzzy experience. However, is it not a requirement to identify a correct diagnosis prior to an appropriate plan of healing? Personally, my response is 'absolutely', causing me to be hesitant to say to another dealing with a negative to, "Forget about it, it is in the past, this is today". Perhaps the issues caused by the trigger being experienced can be adjusted to negate the negative defined and possibly, even, be turned into a positive! I can guarantee that is sometimes possible.

We have no control of the past; we can only control the affect it has on us today... sometimes. I have found that to try to force myself to not have certain triggers is insane! However, I have discovered that, once I have identified certain triggers, I can sometimes control today's page of my life story. For instance, perhaps ten years ago, I was playing a board game that involved a timer, and the players were to accomplish certain tasks prior to the timer going off. The timer was clicking and the tension at the table increasing. I recognized I was becoming extremely agitated but did not understand why, am still not certain today! My opinion of this incident is that I was experiencing a trigger. It was not even my turn; however, I was sweating, shaking, and having trouble breathing. Because playing board games is not a high item on my preference list these days, if I am invited to play a game with which I am not familiar, I ask if a timer is involved in the game. I have chosen not to spend a lot of time trying to get answers regarding this identified issue in my life as it is not affecting meeting my goals nor is it affecting my happiness, nor my daily life. I now recognize that I have the ability to avoid the situation and still be responsible and respectful to all involved, including me. Sometimes, one can control the effects of a recognized trigger by simply avoiding the situation politely.

Other triggers are more difficult. I believe we all, at times, will experience unexpected triggers that may alter our day. However, if I identify a current situation as a trigger, I oftentimes can quickly allow it to pass with just a thought. Remember, you are the one who has some control over how this day's happenings are going to affect your day today. You have the choice to ask about a game you are invited to play, because you have already done your healing work and identified certain information; and only you have the control of you to simply smile because that man who just passed you reminded you of your deceased husband. You choose…you pay the consequences.

SUPPLEMENT to TRIGGERS

1. Are you aware of an expected trigger in your life pertaining to a certain date? If the trigger is one that is bringing negativity into that day, perhaps you can identify a positive you might be able to introduce into that date. Consider a note on the calendar that will help allow you to experience positive on that date.

2. If my definition of triggers makes sense to you, perhaps it may help if you spend time identifying triggers, particularly if you have a life story which you feel dominates much of your life today. If, suddenly, something happens to make you feel as though negativity has entered this day; consider the possibility it may have been some sort of trigger. I have found that the more situations I examined in my past layers; the easier it has been for me to identify when I am experiencing a trigger and why, often allowing it to pass quickly. No need to allow it to control this day if the situation happened in the past and is no longer.

3. If or when you discover something is a trigger to you, which can be as simple a thing as a piece of your clothing, try to discover an action you can take now to control the trigger instead of the trigger controlling you. For instance, you could give the piece of clothing to a shelter across town so you would not see it.

4. I have identified triggers in my life that I cannot control; sometimes, however, I have identified a way for me to be able to control effects on me. If you believe you cannot control the trigger, that's ok. Yesterday you had not yet identified it. Just identifying a negative is important. How can you fix the problem if you have not identified it?

5. If you are ready, write a goal. If not, that's ok. You still need to celebrate; I am certain you are accomplishing more than you are labeling currently!

TRIGGERS ADDENDUM

If you are still overwhelmed with anger/guilt/shame; and the issue you define involves another human; you have a choice: try to change another/change the situation/ allow yourself to be consumed today by the past scenario which cannot be changed because it already happened...or...

Stop, take a deep breath, and consider another option. As a believer, I believe God is never wrong and I believe the Bible. And the Bible says that God has provided us with armor. This might be hard for you to accept right at this moment. But, if you are healing, Satan is angry and probably working to prevent the outcome. You have access to the Sword-of-the-Spirit piece of armor available to quote the Bible at the devil; don't forget that God is at your side and on your side. The devil is the enemy. Come on, is it even possible to name a more powerful Ally than God? But He also gives us freedom to make our own today; some positives and, perhaps some negatives, and we each have the choice to examine... or not.

Looking back today; I think it is possible that each time I was slipping back down on the ladder, I was dealing with spiritual warfare. I would have saved a lot of time on the ladder had I done then what I do today. I simply yell at Satan when I sense his interference in that which I feel directed to do by God. While silently praying, I sometimes sense I can see or hear God's encouragement through the person with whom I am speaking. As you are climbing the ladder, there may be times when you slip back a rung; I experienced that frequently. However, it may help to remember that the Sword of the Spirit (Bible containing words of God) and Prayer are <u>always available</u>... and... <u>neither require standing!!!</u> You can face Satan right now and use them! I encourage you to use both; I am certain you will find it extremely helpful as well as limiting time required on the healing ladder.

Although triggers did not cease when I stepped off the ladder into the Light; I am often amazed as to how God uses them today.

Scenarios triggering only negativity within me in the past; today, often provide positive results. Not only by giving answers to lingering questions for me personally; but, often, by providing additional information helpful to others dealing with like issues. Realizing that I am not alone in experiencing many scenarios, I believe others have pages in life stories that require multiple insights as well as a negating of negative results to heal. Time has been required for God to do all that was necessary for me to not feel the pain if I am triggered or sharing a certain past painful memory. The sources of the pain had to be labeled for me on the ladder. And sometimes remaining steps, unknown to me then, have been identified in surprising ways to alleviate the pain...even if the trigger is presently repeated! Sometimes God shows me that there is still remaining work I need to do on me to accomplish the definition of the believer I wish to be. My prayer for you is that you will also be able to say, as I now do, when you climb off the ladder into the Light that will surround you: The negative is being negated allowing me to now polish up the positive results of the healing that has taken place.

Today, when I am triggered by a previously examined scenario popping into my consciousness; I assume that I need to note what situation I am currently experiencing and wait. Sometimes I pray because I do not understand why 'this' is happening; is it an insight or answer I am to comprehend, or an action I am to take. The result shows me Who was the One always in control. I believe, if I am walking on a path following His lead; my steps will be guided by Him in many different ways. Consequently, I do not experience the trepidation involving triggers that I once had. When a scenario repeats today in my mind that I examined on the ladder, it is truly amazing how the same scenario shows me something entirely different today. At times I have been thankful I was not provided with the current information when struggling with the scenario on the ladder.

One thing I have learned in acquiring a sense of equality to others, is that others within past scenarios may have responded also and may have also been affected: but, very possibly, in a much different manner than I. Today, I have a new goal: that I always examine and respond with the recognition that I only live my life's pages and others only live only their life pages. I have found that, when I act according to that goal, the negative emotive reactions originally present in examining a scenario are not present allowing me a much broader perspective. If my goal is that today's scenario on my life-story page be according to God's will; it is probably required that I act according to His definitions. Experience teaches me too frequently that consequences of me following my choices are not generally pleasant. I trust each time you step up the ladder up to the next rung, you feel encouraged… and a bit changed. It is much easier and faster when I do not try to control everything.

My personal experience is that, although triggers do not control today as in the past, unexpected triggers did not end stepping off the healing ladder onto solid ground surrounded in the Light. In writing these addendums, I am opening my life-story to past pages and often re-experiencing triggers along with experiencing some new scenarios. Currently I believe God uses memories associated with past triggers to show me something He wishes me to 'lean into' allowing me to be beneficial in this day. I have discovered that the new insight will not only be helpful when talking to another regarding his/her abuse; but is also helpful in my personal daily routine. It is often obvious to me that my reactions living in today and triggered by past scenarios are much different than when I first studied the event. 'Surviving' a day and 'living' a day are quite different in many respects. Which I would define as another gift God provides to His followers… if chosen to accept.

HEALING LADDER

Sometimes, when I am conscious of having failed on a step in my healing, it feels as though I am on a ladder and have slipped down a rung. Thus, I liken the healing process to a healing ladder. Twenty-five years ago, I found myself in what I have since described as a dark pit; I could not stand up. It was as though I was struggling in a pool of black muck and I was unsuccessfully trying to almost stand, at least get my hands up at waist level, before slipping and falling into the muck again. All I could see was darkness. I do not believe there was a sound as I was only aware of my presence in the place and, consequently felt totally alone and helpless. At times I literally screamed at God that I could not feel Him. At one point, however, I was able to discover a way out. Because I was in a pit, I had to go up. When I felt the ladder, I started the climb from the darkness of the pit towards the Light I am walking in today. But, first, I had to be able to stand. If one stays prone on the ground; climbing a ladder is a grim, if not impossible, expectation.

However, once one has accomplished the ability to stand, defining and placing a foot on the first rung of the ladder becomes a possibility if one chooses to do so. Once on a ladder, one is moving in an upward motion and into a brighter place, assuming he/she is climbing out of a pit. I felt as though, after accomplishing the first few rungs of the ladder, I could not only recognize and use an inner strength I did not know was available to me; but I seemed to also start seeing a small shaft of Light that would broaden and brighten with each successive rung on the ladder. For me, oftentimes as I hung on tightly and fought to stay on the ladder, the Light was definable as an awareness of the presence of my Savior allowing me to realize I was not alone even though I was in a very personal struggle.

SUPPLEMENT to HEALING LADDER

1. Screaming was helpful to me. It was, no doubt, not a necessity for Him to be able to hear me, however.

2. If you feel screaming may benefit you, allow me to offer some suggestions; I know they work well as I have tried them out! Be sure no others, such as children, neighbors, or pets, are in a place to hear the screams. I would turn the radio or television volume way up. Scream to your heart's delight. If you feel like something physical would help; perhaps getting on a treadmill would be a plan.

3. I discovered when I was broken, physical activity helped, particularly with anger issues; I needed to do something that took strength to accomplish. In the middle of the night, I took rags from the ragbag, particularly if they had seams, and ripped and ripped and ripped. I remember using the tactic in my pre-teen and teen years also. Perhaps there are some chores that need to be accomplished around your property. If it is raining, perhaps you could move the furniture around.

4. Look for something within your current environment which may help you calm down and alter an undesired mood. It has helped me to walk far away from others into a cherished environment and sing favorite hymns while looking at the scenes around me. Maybe it would help you. By the way, I have noticed that animals and trees do not appear to be bothered by the sour notes I tend to expound during such times.

HEALING-LADDER ADDENDUM

My suggestion to the 'victim' is to ask yourself questions when studying past scenarios, and to keep climbing. However, you may discover, as did I, that you are studying the scenarios differently and for different reasons. The present may become much more important to you than trying to understand the past. My experience and the time required on each ladder rung was changing as I was beginning to feel bogged down with the questioning and negativity that I recognized was not helping me experience the current day I desired. So, maybe it is time to consider changing the meds? I decided (unfortunately much higher on the ladder than this) that studying the scenarios as the 'victim' in each scenario increased my confusion and anger.

The scenarios I examined generally involved family. The common result of my questioning significant others was more negativity, as others in the scenarios were not currently making the same choices as I. I discovered that they defined the scene differently than I if they remembered the scenario. Because I was turning to them; the bitterness and anger was being stirred within them and I had the ladle in my hand! This method was not providing me with the results I desired and was extremely hurtful to all. So, I would like to share the positive I was able to identify when personally examining familial scenarios. Because the people within the scenarios were also within my past daily life, I knew some history of each. At least enough to allow me to 'step out of me and become them in the scenario'. I tried to experience the same scenario from the others' perspectives. The understanding of the total scenarios I have gained by doing this on the following rungs is truly amazing! I also suggest considering always turning to God for clarity and help before starting the process. God waited a long time for me to lean into the knowledge that He is the ONE with a greater understanding than anyone else, including me. But, when I did......WOW!!!

The more I was identifying the cost to me of staying in the past with my studying, trying to make 2+2=4 within each scenario; my end goals were starting to become more positive. As I felt stronger, my goals started to be redefined to include a change within me. … So, how about changing me so today's scenarios would change? I decided to let them deal with them and I would work on dealing with just me. I now can easily define this as the time when I started to search for methods to allow me to feel more 'equal' to others. I was recognizing that living by the definitions of me in the abuse was not conducive to aiding in getting me to where I was deciding I wanted to be. I was becoming strong enough to claim my choices rather than allowing other humans to continue controlling my choices; convincing me slowly that yes, perhaps I could feel equal to others in my environment.

Believers believe that all are equal at the foot of the cross. We are children of God. He has a path for each of us to follow to accomplish His will for us. Could the strength to accept and act upon these beliefs possibly be a prerequisite for a past 'victim' to have the ability to follow God's leading on His path for her/him protected by His armor? If so, would this be a good reason for me as a helper to have the other lead the conversations dictating topics to discuss? Is not the one who experienced the story the best to identify and define the present consequences of same?

In my life today looking at a past scenario that a trigger has brought to my mind out of the blue, I am interested in identifying if/how it is preventing me from following His will today. The bitterness, anger, and desire for revenge is no longer taking up space on the page, generally. If it is, however, then I work on identifying the negative and how it can be changed into a positive for me to be able to help another. Generally, a conversation soon comes up allowing me to share the experience for another to use in some way helpful to them. So, keep climbing and tweaking my suggestions hopefully enabling you to say the same when you step off the ladder. I admit, it is not always easy for me to live reflecting what I say I believe; but when I stop, take a deep breath, and choose to put forth the effort do so, it is a positive in some manner.

As you continue the climb examining and tweaking what works for you to experience positivity on each rung, I believe God is right beside you. I believe HE has a plan for each of us and desires to be our constant Ally. You may not feel strong enough to stand on a battlefield in this world yet...I didn't at this point in my healing, but HE is ready to answer the questions which will keep you on the path HE has for you. Hopefully, you will choose much earlier than I to turn to Him and the gifts you have from Him as your constant Ally in the process. It is an immense help to know that He has got me...and you...covered!

In the Bible Paul describes a piece of the armor God provides His believers to do just that! It helps me personally, not only to envision Jesus standing right next to me when I feel as though I am standing on that battlefield, but to realize I am covered by the shield of faith that He provides. It is described as covering the armor and, standing behind it, we believers are covered when facing the enemy surrounded by the protection of Christ. My experience tells me that, when I lean into my faith, I also sense a strength and acknowledge a description of self, allowing me to accomplish the job I believe He has put in front of me. And, because the shield of faith obviously has me all covered defensively facing the devil, I am able to use the concrete sword against him with my body protected from anything he may be throwing at me. I know it works because I use this regularly in my life today bringing a sense of peace and feeling of safety that I never had before my experience on the healing-ladder, including experiences with new _and_ old triggers.

I also have discovered that I do not stand alone in experiencing unexpected answers to past questions. And I am guessing it will be your experience also. Following the steps on the rungs of this ladder, I did get many insights; however still had some lingering questions. Not everything has been answered by this day; but once I realized I had the strength to live in this day with the past story closed on the shelf, I find the unanswered questions do not hold the importance they once did. Experience has also taught me to believe fully that, if I follow God's direction instead of mine; whatever the end brings with each question will allow me to live in the present with a sense of peace. You may have more questions, as I did, working on the ladder steps. Looking back on the climb to the Light, it makes sense that gaining answers provides a clearer picture in addition to broader definitions beyond me. Comprehending the whole picture beyond me personally, was extremely helpful in negating the overpowering negative emotions. You may discover the same and note you are making changes in goals. I can say, for me it was, and remains today, a fascinating experience. I am still recognizing these gifts provided as I strive to follow HIS leading. I am certain you will have many of the same experiences as you experience the climb.

My faith tells me the Holy Spirit is with me every second of every day and night. And, fellow believer, I believe He is with you… this minute and every other. He knows your story better than you do. He 'gets it'. What a gift you have as a believer by choosing to have your faith. Perhaps it may help you feel your strength concretely to again remember how God feels about you; enabling you to continue climbing:

Romans 8:38-39: *"For I am convinced that neither death nor life, neither angels nor demons, neither the present nor the future, nor any powers, neither height nor depth, nor anything else in all creation, will be able to separate us from the love of God that is in Christ Jesus our Lord."* (NIVp1228)

Romans 8:28: *"And we know that in all things God works for the good of those who love him, who have been called according to his purpose."* (NIVp1228)

The message of Calvary is God's love for you and for me. A message written in red with the blood of Jesus Christ.

PUZZLE

While slipping around in the muck in the darkness, I could not think of anything beyond getting up and out of the pit. Once I felt I was climbing up, however, I began to compare my search for answers to working a jigsaw puzzle. I will often waste time trying to force a piece to fit where it does not belong. Consequently, I am forced to change my mind when the piece does not change, I must change. A process, I discovered, much like the healing process in which I felt as though I was defining puzzle pieces fitting into a big picture that I, at a future time, could identify and would then understand how all the pieces fit. When I began to see the past situations more clearly, I began to also understand why I was at the place I currently found myself in the healing process. Then I could proceed to the next step by making the necessary changes in me. I cannot change the shape of the puzzle pieces, nor the past situations, I can only change me in this day and in tomorrow.

Various times in my life, prior to my pit experience, I would realize I was questioning why I was in a certain position or experiencing a given emotion creating a state of confusion. Then my life would cause an interruption in my thinking that may last for months or years because my normal life was all consuming. While experiencing the darkness of the pit however, the situation reversed; and my daily life responsibilities interrupted the consumable experience of the pit.

My personal realization as I began to achieve the goals of each ladder rung was a gift of a new sense of clarity, also offering an excellent reason for celebration. Possibly, the discoveries also offered me a piece that fit into the big unknown picture that was necessary for me to identify before I could meet my goals. Clarity always helped me define the next ladder rung.

Any puzzle causes one to be confused. For me, a jigsaw puzzle on a table in front of me presents a threat of sorts; perhaps why I liken the healing process to defining puzzle pieces and then fitting them together to form a big picture. The more pieces I can identify and fit into other pieces correctly, the clearer the overall big picture becomes.

I identified the big picture that was emerging as my life story. The past situations are the little puzzles I had to understand before I could determine why the big puzzle was making the picture it does as I fit the pieces from all the little puzzles into the big one. The pieces I identified on the ladder were already formed and could not be changed; meaning that, if I felt content with the picture they were forming, it was not necessary to make any changes in me to change the current life picture.

When I finally stepped off the healing ladder for the first time onto solid ground surrounded in the Light, it was much easier to stand back out of the big picture. Doing so allowed me to realize that the puzzle picture of my life story did not have the painful effect it had earlier in the healing process. I was able to identify nuances which were always present but not identified because I did not have access to the tools I have today with which to lessen confusion. With the understanding of how the puzzle pieces fit together as I studied the various situations in my past, I found it fascinating that the only way I was able to describe it was: 'God thing'.

SUPPLEMENT to PUZZLE

1. Do you think it could be possible there are secrets unidentifiable to you within your living environment or within the puzzles you are currently identifying, or may be examining higher up on your ladder, that may prevent you from labeling necessary pieces allowing you to see the total picture? If so, it is ok. I have lots of pieces I cannot identify in my big picture as well as identifying secrets encompassing my childhood; however, I define myself today as living in the Light on solid ground. Occasionally, some incident, or a friend familiar with my story, will define another piece from a past situation that seemingly fits an empty spot on the big puzzle that shows my life story. Think about it this way: Even if you identify every piece from every past situation you choose to examine and discover how each piece fits into the big picture; there are still blank areas in the big picture because you are still writing your life story today. The thing is, that is good; because you have some control in how this day is written! So, how about a smile?

2. My experience on the healing ladder has given me the gift that: It is now more important for me on this day to concentrate on today being a positive day than it is to define the remaining puzzle pieces in the piles from the past. I did not have a clue where to start healing initially. I am, today, twenty-five years into the healing work I am describing in this book. To get to this place, I examined countless problematic situations, each with various piles of pieces requiring identification to understand the puzzle the situation revealed. I believe it was this process that helped me arrive at the place I am currently; or maybe I should say will be when I finish this project and choose to close my book again, put it back on the shelf and turn around to step into tomorrow.

3. It was interesting to note as I climbed the ladder examining pertinent puzzles along the way; oftentimes familiar connections would become apparent. The clarity these tools were providing began indicating to me that my Savior was always present. The latter puzzles from my adulthood layers of my book involving important situations that did not have the conclusion I was fighting for at the time, revealed a picture showing me I could say: "I'm sure glad that situation didn't turn out the way I was hoping it would at the time!"

4. If you can identify with anything in this section, check to see if your puzzle shows you something about yourself that you can possibly change to take any negativity out of today or tomorrow.

5. Always remember, you can only change you, not any other. Remember to celebrate the headway you have made in your healing process. Always celebrate what you accomplish! This process was not a big warm fuzzy for me and you probably feel the same. I found identifying and leaning into some positive on each ladder rung is extremely important. You may reach the same conclusion.

6. You may want to consider dating all you write. Doing so allowed me to have many reasons to celebrate looking back over past notes indicating the many positives achieved. Trust me, if you continue tweaking the following chapters and writing your goals, you can expect more positive changes in your definitions and goals! So, take time for five deep breaths.

PUZZLE ADDENDUM

When putting the pieces of a puzzle together, it is a requirement to not only examine the piece in your hand but others determining how they fit together to complete the big picture. If I only look at the piece I am holding, and nothing else, I will probably never be able to see the whole picture. With each evaluation, I would have accomplished more faster if I would have prayed. Each piece needs to fit in correctly to the other pieces for the big picture to be clear. After all, the One who knows which and how each piece fits into the puzzle, is currently right beside you, right? However, might it be helpful if, while on the ladder, one recognizes <u>He also has the definition of the future</u>! .... One possible argument to not question His timing as to when my questions are answered? After all, does it not make sense that when the last puzzle piece is placed in the proper space, my life in this world has ended?

Standing on the Foundation in the Light, I realized that I was still healing; however, the 'process' had changed. My self-identification was changing allowing me to define the scenarios making up the big picture with more clarity. And I also I realized how often the negativity in the puzzle pieces could be turned into a positive to use in this day. Throughout the early years, my group of friends often heard me sharing frustrations regarding certain puzzle pieces that seemed to be in the right position but still did not provide a clear picture to me. What I did not realize when originally questioning but believe today, is that various clarities that I now accept as answering my questions would have knocked me off the ladder when I was initially asking them. My definition of the person I was when climbing the ladder varies from the person I define standing on the Foundation and turning from the pit. I now recognize that I have experienced the fact that God's timing offers better results than making decisions according to my defined timing. I also recognize I have a strength today that I did not have at my disposal when hanging onto the ladder.

One of the biggest reasons I thank God readily in this day for my life story is that I did not have some troubling answers when I reached the top rung of the ladder and crawled onto the foundation and stood. Walking is a quite different experience than is climbing, and the ability to stand is required. Consequently, when on the Foundation, we are covered by the armor of God! The total view of everything and the affect it had on me changed when I climbed out of the pit. I realized I had the power to act that I did not have on the ladder. In the pit, I did not have the option to close the book, put it on the shelf and turn into today. The ladder experience provided the tools offering me the ability in this day to turn past negatives into positives to be polished in the puzzle piece available (perhaps even required to use, if on the path following His lead today). I believe anyone on the ladder may have the opportunity in the future to experience the same. Sometimes, I believe I am taught that there are certain things I am required to 'experience' before I can 'get it' as an aid to use when following His path for my life. My current goal is to be on the path following the directions of the One who holds the definition of my future. He was there on my climb out of the pit also not allowing me to experience every answer I desired; for which I am, today, extremely thankful! I no longer experience the desire and frustration of unanswered questions bringing negativity into the present.

You may have already experienced being triggered unexpectedly with information about your life that was previously absent or forgotten. An example could be a child who is at the age you were when you experienced the forgotten, perhaps a phone call from another you identify as a stranger, or a stranger who looks familiar and causes you to have an inexplicable sensation. When this happens, you have a puzzle in front of you because you experienced something you cannot explain. You have some information, but not the full story. A desire to define what the whole big picture shows is what causes one to locate the pieces to the puzzle and then fit the pieces together. It is possible the big picture may make your life story less cloudy for you by answering some questions.

The end goal in a jigsaw puzzle is to fit all the pieces together to clearly see the total picture. However, any jigsaw puzzle I have seen has the picture on the box. I did not have that advantage when I began the healing process. My healing-ladder experience was forced upon me by an unexpected trigger. A trigger that I describe as experiencing a dam break crashing over me forcing snippets of memories from years past to be thrashing into my whole body resulting in open wounds of negative emotions, questions, and confusion. The trigger that caused the dam to break and changed my life drastically was standing at a casket looking down at my main abuser throughout my childhood. As I was looking at him lying in the casket, I became aware of strange emotions taking over my body. The dam broke and I dropped to the floor next to the casket with no control whatsoever. Prior to that experience, when living in my childhood home, I was aware of being extremely uncomfortable around him and feeling unsafe when in his presence. If asked, and answered honestly, I may have said that I hated him; although I understood that I, as a believer, felt required to love him. At the time of the funeral, I did not live in the same area and had no to little contact after my high-school graduation twenty-nine years earlier when I turned from the home in which I was raised and walked into the city to get a job with the desire to become somebody else.

Throughout those twenty-nine years, my goal was to live a totally different life in a different world than I had in the past. Today, I recognize that choices I made during those years prior to the healing-ladder experience, caused my life to be a daily struggle to say that I had accomplished my goal as an adult. An adult who intermittently sensed I lacked a clear definition of my current as well as past life. Particularly when I experienced infrequent but menacing questions and inexplicable triggers. The unanswered questions presented one unidentified definition of my problem; after all, I was not living the past life. My argument declared I had some control as I was following my own directions. One being to avoid anything 'religious' as much as possible. I was a believer having been methodically taught the rules of loving and obeying one's parents, forgiveness, self-recognition as a sinner resulting in God always watching me to see when I needed to be punished for sins I committed. The people I called mom and dad were church deacon and deaconess. Consequently, whenever I experienced something from the past, I chose to 'stuff it' turning away into the present life I made for myself. One which allowed me self-identification as a member of those people who, throughout my childhood, I only looked up to with a type of wonder. (A choice that caused my life to be one that I would identify today as surviving, rather than simply thriving.) But I had college degrees, lived in a nice house in a nice neighborhood, ate and danced in fancy places in fancy clothes; thus, had met <u>my</u> goal. I tried to do all I could when alone to not spend time trying to figure out what was wrong with my life; after all, I was living a different life as a different person; all I had to do was look around for verification.

I am fully aware of the fact that I do not stand alone in many or all my life's stories. Today, I am typing this believing I am following God's leading in doing so. I can honestly state that I am thankful for my life story as it has allowed me to share these healing-ladder experiences with others allowing them to tweak and apply; hopefully helping them meet their end goals. And, in a lot less time than I has taken me because of many poor choices I made over the years that others reading will hopefully avoid.

If you have a few pieces of the puzzle in your hand, it is impossible to define the total picture. The total picture requires each piece fitting into another correctly, requiring you to keep 'looking beyond'. If you are experiencing the emotional results of discoveries and answers that I was at this point; it is impossible for you to have a clue as to what the total picture is. If the trigger creates negativity within you; it is likely impossible, immediately, to 'look beyond' yourself. If you are like I, you are on the floor unable to stand and being bombarded with inexplicable snippets of memories showing uncomfortable mysteries 'out of the blue'.

Prior to putting a puzzle together, the box needs to be open and the pieces <u>available</u> and <u>identified</u>. At this point, one has choices.

Before the dam break, my choice was to not open the box trying to pretend nothing 'weird' was happening when I experienced what I now recognize as the 'nudges' God was giving me. As a believer, I can guarantee you I am <u>certain</u> God was with me during those twenty-nine years when I was consciously ignoring Him striving for a control of my life. Because I chose that path instead of following His lead; I am also positive (without knowing the result of the 'unchosen choice') that my life story would have been different in those years. Today, believing I am following His path, each day is more positive than in that period of my life. And, today, my fancy clothes are hanging in a closet that is seldom opened unless I require a light bulb from the shelf above them.

The other choice one has is to open the box (mine had a title on it: "My Life Story") and pick up the pieces one at a time. Each piece must be identified and examined. Thus, an important requirement is the ability to look beyond each piece to all others. The requirement for that box to be opened may be for one to experience the path God has chosen for him/her to follow. But, regardless of the stated reason for opening the box, the puzzle pieces must be identified, understood, and connected to gain clarity as to what the big picture shows. As believers, access to God's leading with prayer is available with each piece of the puzzle in the box. Only two beings will have experienced the total finished picture that will be available. I cannot speak for you, but I can guarantee you that I was not the One while working on my personal puzzle with every answer. But had I chosen to allow God, with each piece, to direct me; the process would have taken less time, probably in years! Each puzzle piece may bring unexpected factors into the procedure that require addressing. In my experience, negative emotions, inability to 'look beyond' me, and turning to other humans instead of God lengthened my time on the ladder.

If a puzzle piece is on the floor, or thrown into the garbage, the total picture will never be identified. Self-honesty is a requirement for one's correct story to be on the table. Generally, I found, in self-examination, that I did not like what I discovered about me. It was sometimes hard to <u>not</u> throw that insight in the garbage. Consequently, it was when I was putting a new piece in the puzzle, that I often would adjust my goals while on the ladder. If a piece is destroyed the picture will never be completed and a wound may not be identified nor healed.

It was important for me to remember, while working on the puzzle, that I still had a life to live with responsibilities involving others to fulfill. Turning to God and seeing more of the Light with each rung of the ladder enabled me to look beyond self and begin to negate the negative and recognize the possibility of positive. I began to realize Who it is in control of all. Today I realize that I had to continue to follow God's lead as I was not yet ready to get all the information I wanted. It is also fascinating in this day to recognize that when a scenario that I examined initially and put into place comes back to mind, my total response to the piece is much more positive. God helped me to be able to look at the puzzle pieces from perspectives other than just mine. Because family members were included in the big picture I was putting together, I had information I would not have had with strangers. If your pieces include people who you knew well, you may choose to try erasing any trigger you experience and study the scenario on the piece from each of <u>their</u> perspectives. It is a tool I use that allows me today to 'fight their case' instead of mine. Using information that I know about them, I try to 'be them' in the puzzle piece that has triggered me. The more often I do it, the easier it becomes. The result, for me, has been a negating of past negativity and a polishing of positive. It surprises me how often today, if a past page is open in front of me, that my reaction is often totally different than before. Confusion is limited because I often look at a puzzle piece and say aloud: "I get it". Consequently, today, I can honestly state that I am thankful for my life story. I also believe I would not have been able to make this statement today without the choice to turn to follow God's guidance, rather than mine.

CLAIM IT

I have learned that I am the only adult I can change in my life story and I had to do exactly that to meet my end goal of 'Be Happy'. Initially, I did not have access to the tools because I had not identified them, nor had I claimed them.

The idea of claiming is especially important in my personal healing process; it means to me that if I need to claim it, then I am responsible for it. It is mine, not yours, nor his, nor hers, but mine. For instance, I claim my definition of my life story; but I will not claim the definition of your life story as I recognize it is not mine to claim. Just as I also recognize my life-story definition is not yours to claim. It has been <u>extremely</u> important for me, personally, to use the word claim this way in my healing process.

When I began recognizing I had been claiming responsibilities in situations I should not have been claiming; like guilt, for instance, the big picture became a valuable tool in providing me understanding rather than confused questioning. I then could identify clear, concrete steps helping me change myself to be a better, healthier person using the knowledge that I am the only adult I am able to change.

SUPPLEMENT to CLAIM IT

1. Proper claiming is a concept always, in my opinion, one to consider when struggling to solve a puzzle. Perhaps with the situation currently in your thinking, you could look at the concepts you have identified as pertinent in the picture, labels such as blame, responsibility, and action and list them.

2. In looking at your list, identify the labels that pertain to you. Remember, you can only change you; but are you able to change something you cannot identify? If blame is on the list, do you feel blame for the situation you are examining? Look at the whole picture the puzzle is making. Studying the other characters, listen to what they say and watch silent body language. Are you accepting or claiming your responsibility in the situation? Or are you recognizing that you are accepting blame that you should not be taking? Did you take something that was misguided to you and you accepted the label? Whatever issue is in any puzzle you examine, it may be as beneficial for you as it has been for me to look at what you, personally, claimed in that situation because you may learn you have consistently in your life-story layers claimed a misguided label, like blame, guilt, responsibility, fault that was not yours to claim. Remembering that you can only change you … If you find that you have done this; you may decide to check to see if you are still doing it without having labeled it.

3. Before you write a goal, check for an issue that is possibly something you readily claim unreasonably, and you label it as unhealthy or toxic. Then, you may choose to write a goal to stop claiming misguided_____. It may be possible that certain situations or individuals are consistently connected to this issue; perhaps not. However, please realize here and now that you can only change you, not another adult. And, that you are responsible to pay consequences for your choices. (I know because I have hurt significant others by <u>not</u> following this advice at this point in my personal healing experience!)

4. You may recognize, as I often do today, that you did <u>not</u> claim a label for which you <u>were</u> responsible in the past scenario. Does this revelation require an action from you currently? If so, you may choose to write a goal allowing another celebration upon completion.

5. You may recognize a recurring pattern in something as you examine more and more puzzle pieces and decide it to be significant for you to watch for it, as you begin fitting the various pieces into the big puzzle. You may find, if you change you when these same people or situations are repeated, you are also able to control how you are affected by any negativity the situation causes. I have found that, if certain situations repeat consistently and I make changes in me, the negative effects are greatly reduced in my present day.

6. Celebrate your discoveries!

CLAIM-IT ADDENDUM

If your goal is to heal from an abusive situation, you may be dealing with overpowering emotions and feeling very alone as you try to change the results affecting you today; I felt like that many times on my ladder climb. The word 'claim' could cause one to consider throwing this book in the garbage right now. Please do not do that...especially if you have already recognized positives. My life story has taught me that had I turned to God early on for clarity and answers, many more years of my life would be labeled today as 'thriving' rather than 'surviving'. I am not a doctor; however, I do think if I have a sore thumb and choose a pill for a sore throat, or choose to ignore the pain, neither choice will help the thumb much. In fact, the thumb may become worse... and thumbs are connected to the hand. The consequences I pay years later, just might be dependent on the choice I make today. Maybe turning to Another who has always been there is in order... One who loves me, defines me as an equal to others, and already has all the answers, perhaps?

Here is what I believe my turning to Him has, and still is today, teaching me personally about 'claiming' as I strive to not act and make decisions today according to <u>my</u> conclusions. Please note that I did not state in the prior sentence that I always act and make decisions today by turning to Him; sometimes it is still difficult. But when I act in accordance with what I SAY I believe and look beyond me, my current life's day is <u>not</u> determined by my past-story pages.

Ok...here we go...

I have read and agree that it is not uncommon for one family member to be the 'victim'. If your story involves an 'abuser' who is/was a family member or a 'significant other' to family members, it may be difficult for other family members to support, or even to believe your story. There may be secrets not known to all; but, likely affecting all. Just because others are on a puzzle piece with you; you cannot assume their puzzle piece would be described by them akin to yours. Please allow me to explain one of the many lessons I learned in my healing process if you are currently dealing with this situation as a victim or a helper to another:

Today it is extremely important for me to claim what is mine to claim always remembering that others who share an experience in my life are as unique an individual as am I. I believe that consequences of decisions I made early in my healing process involving significant others added negativity in all our lives. When I was on the healing ladder, I turned to significant others who were in my life often present on the puzzle pieces I was examining for answers to questions and clarity I was seeking. Not only did I not realize at the time that their puzzle piece may not look exactly as mine does even if we were both in the same scenario; but I did not stop to think they may have made different choices involving those past puzzle pieces.

A conversation with a family member describing one of my puzzle pieces that include an abuse I experienced verified this conclusion. The member was defining the situation exactly as I had defined the scenario years earlier when I was climbing the ladder; except my abuse was not a part of this member's description of the event. Although this member was emotional and expressing confusion, my abuse was not a part of the puzzle piece being described. I also define both of us as believers. We shared the scenario reacting to it and defining it differently not making either of us wrong or right; but different. My family member surprised me by bringing this incident up in a conversation forming questions thirty-seven years after the incident happened; obviously triggered negatively as was I when I examined it on the ladder. I also concluded that we feel very differently about the other family members in the same scenario. I do not hold the opinion, however, that one of us is wrong and one is right... simply different. I also believe that, today, we define my abuser differently as we experienced different lives with him in our past life-story pages.

I believe God was with us that night we were together conversing. And I believe there were many lessons in that conversion for me to claim on a very personal level. One is that individuals make different choices regarding a shared experience that affect how each reacts to the shared experience years later. It taught me that other humans, even if they shared an experience, describing it as I do, may not have the capacity to provide clarity for me. We shared the same incident for a portion of one day on our life pages and then, individually, turned from one another into the rest of our lives. I question how that night's conversation would have been different had I realized when on the healing-ladder rungs that each family member was unique and making individual life choices each day and each of us would also experience consequences of those choices. I hurt this family member and probably many others by interrupting their daily lives with my calls when I started my ladder climb. I still, today, pay the consequences for choosing to not turn to the One who knows not only my past and present, but also my future. Only One was with each of us that whole day and every other of our individual lives. Consequently, even if I, as a helper am with another who shares like experiences to mine, I claim a personal responsibility to be careful to not define any requirements. Because we are unique individuals with not one identical life-story page. I have been in a situation that leads me to believe I would apply the same goal to identical twins within a given family who I could not call by the correct name until I 'knew' them personally and individually for an extended period of time.

That night's conversation with my family member helped me immensely to be able to look beyond me also. I was then, and am further yet this day, removed from the place I was in the shared scenario that night but also, who I was when initially climbing the healing ladder. I did not share my puzzle-description in our conversation. I had hurt this family member over and over with my question years prior to this conversation. I was at a different place when listening; I was able to see beyond me that evening. I was not the one questioning that night. I had been living a new life after examining my puzzle pieces for ten years when that conversation took place. We each have a life-story page involving the same incident. Our individual pages that night, and no doubt are still, very different. I doubt anyone could convince me that either one of us were lying then nor would be lying today when describing that experience differently.

Do I believe you have the right to be angry that you were abused?... Absolutely. Do I believe I had the right to be angry that I was a victim? ... Absolutely. But I discovered that the anger, guilt, victim self- identification, blah blah, were zapping me of strength required to climb the ladder successfully and in less time. I discovered the ladder-rung assignments I was giving myself in examining pieces were triggering stuffed emotions. However, I also discovered defining and claiming the emotions was enabling necessary goals to be identified allowing negating negativity and polishing positivity for future days. I discovered that I had no control to change the past-puzzle piece; but that the examinations gave me information required to make necessary changes allowing me to define what I did or did not claim. I had more control in the current day. I also realized that I would pay, in the future, the consequences of the choices I claimed in each day on the ladder. And I was beginning to realize differences in experiencing the ladder climb when I turned to the ONE who 'gets' me; was and still is, with me on each life-story page, and knows the future.

If consequences are connected to choices, then does it not make sense to look at choices when examining methods and results available with each puzzle piece? I am the one who experiences the consequences of my choices and I am the one striving to meet the goals. One decision I made early on the ladder was to seek counseling for the first time in my life. I chose to go to someone who allowed me to tape the sessions. (I expect to always make this a requirement anytime I am choosing a counselor. I also have received permission to tape conversations involving challenging issues.) I did it because I had learned it is totally amazing what I discovered about me listening to the tape alone with a prayer for guidance and my self-counselor approach. I listened for things I 'say from the gut', generally a quick response to a question. Listening to the tape while commuting back and forth to work or meetings, I have pulled the car off to the side of the road, rewound the tape and said out loud: "What did I say?". Obviously, I was forced to claim what I said; but also, the next important self-question to claim was, "Why would I say that?". It is amazing what I learned about me; sometimes it took a few weeks to figure it out. But the gift I believe it gave me was that it prevented bad decisions I would have made at the time I was taping, or later. Decisions based on unidentified thoughts, emotions, etc. that were obviously affecting me and causing me to answer the way I did, without thinking about it first.

I am the only one experiencing my life story. If you and I lived together every day of our lives, I believe our life stories would still not be identical on each page. I am the only human who has each of my pages so I am the only one with the information that can explain why I said what I did on taped conversations. There were times when I have said listening to such a tape: "I didn't know I feel that way...wow!" Here is my conclusion about taping counseling sessions or conversations like the following paragraph describes: When involved in a conversation in which I am currently reacting to a negative trigger in my life story, I am hurting and not carefully monitoring myself or what I say. I am in this conversation because I know I need help. If I answer quickly, I believe that is when the answer likely comes from the 'gut' not the 'brain', therefore I have not 'tweaked it'. Consequently, if I pay close attention to those answers, I learn the most about me. I would advise anyone to tape and listen to it carefully after because, upon then taking some time to label whatever was the reason for the unexpected response I had made, I also gained additional concrete information helping me to have a better life today. I believe I would have, unknowingly, made decisions that would have created more negativity in my life had I not claimed such discoveries. I cannot define your emotions; but when I am feeling broken or experiencing certain emotions, I do not remember whole conversations. I think it is possible that the conversation pieces I do not remember, are the most important parts to identify enabling me to experience positive rather than repeat past negativity.

I was with a friend from my past recently, and she asked me to tell her what I remembered about her husband's funeral years before. (When this man died, their oldest child was in the third grade). I replied I was hesitant because my memory of the funeral did not really make sense. She said that she felt the same and asked again. We discovered and agreed that we were verifying each other's snippets and thoughts. We also agreed on a conclusion: It is entirely possible that God does not allow us to have memories of some things in our lives until we are at a place when we can 'handle it'. This conversation made it easier to help her these days to be in the present and appreciate experiencing the positive being offered in this current day. This conclusion has allowed me to no longer spend time searching for answers I do not have regarding my past-story pages. My experiences have shown me that sometimes answers are provided in the current day in totally unexpected ways, sometimes not even defined immediately, because the question was not in my current thoughts!

As believers, we have free will <u>and</u> the ability to choose. If I experience anxiety today, my goal is to pray and then make the choice to try and identify any negativity within me, claim it as mine, and deal with it allowing me to label and experience positive for the current day. My experience is that a puzzle piece may come to mind in this day to teach me an unidentified lesson permitting unexpected positivity in this day. Today, I can honestly say...for the most part... that I no longer experience anger from my childhood years because I believe I 'get it'. I defined and claimed choices allowing me to start thinking 'beyond me' as I examined puzzle pieces. Today, if I recognize I am experiencing anger in a 'victim manner'; it is when I feel a current health issue may be a result of past abuse. But, even then, the anger does not control me as it did before I identified these tools on the ladder climb that I still find helpful today and am generally able to apply immediately dissipating the negative.

It was at this ladder rung that I realized I had an important decision to make that would affect present, and probably future, days of my life. Studying the past scenarios on various pieces resulted in varying emotions; some became recurring. I think an example might have been: "oh, they are in this one; so today I'll probably be crazy with anger/sad/put down/blah blah all day after studying this piece". Recognizing such patterns caused me to think about my approaches in studying the pieces searching for answers and insights. I began to question if how I studied each puzzle piece I had in my hand while on the ladder, could not only impact my general attitude that day; but also, future days. Many scenarios were coming to mind with puzzle pieces. And I discovered the way I examined them was affecting my present life upon turning from the puzzle. The emotions I had driving the car, the dogs barking, seemed different when I had examined pieces differently. I began to start identifying less 'pity' of self as well as frustration with self-identity of worthlessness.

Taking some time in this thinking, I concluded that each time I picked up a puzzle piece or had a trigger; I also had a choice: Do I stay the victim or become a survivor? Keeping my goals in mind, the opinions I reached regarding this choice were: If I choose to lean into the 'victim role' in the present day, I will probably be examining each puzzle piece only studying me in the pictures. People reacting to my story may buy me a cup of coffee or take me to lunch and tell me how sorry they feel for me. I will certainly be feeling sorry for me. However, I also realized the 'victim' choice did not seem to lead into the goal of being a different person leading a different life than the 'me' I was examining on the puzzle piece in my hand. At minimum it would probably not improve my self-concept (also an important concept that needed tracking). I was generally already listening to what was being said in scenario pieces, as some questions were being addressed that way. Sometimes a reaction from another would be noted; but from <u>my</u> point of view; resulting in something like "and they made me feel_____"/ "they really hurt me" blah blah blah.

Because I had a job, I could afford a cup of coffee and a lunch occasionally, and I decided I would not accept the self-identification fitting a 'victim'. I wanted to be strong. I knew from experience accepting that I was not equal to others and unworthy offered absolutely nothing to improve life in any day, of any month, in any year. I also discovered that, for me, if an examination of a piece resulted in my feeling the 'victim'; I had studied the piece only looking at me. The feelings I had, my pain, my anger, my guilt... poor me. My conclusion was that choice did nothing to help achieve goals I had for my life. That was a definition of me on <u>the past</u> pages of my life story; and I cannot change that. But was I still claiming it...was my approach leaning into claiming the victim definition for this day and future?

I decided that along with the picture each piece provided, was a choice to examine the piece differently. A tool I realized I preferred using was trying to 'erase me' and to study each scenario from the 'significant others' perspectives. I learned a lot about <u>me</u> (not all positive) using this approach. I also discovered various traits I needed to claim as mine that I had not recognized. Not only has this tool been pivotal in reducing … sometimes even negating... anger and guilt, but it also helped to claim a different definition of me today as well as my views regarding the 'significant others'. I realized on the healing-ladder that I would strive to choose 'survivor' over 'victim'. I wanted a self-definition that includes strength and has worth. If your puzzle involves abuse, self-concept may need to be identified with each piece. I also recognize, today, that it would have been helpful for me to consistently recognize, throughout the healing process, to whom I was leaning for help in defining me and what I was required to claim in each piece I examined. Not only the what but the how was important for me to label. The importance of claiming of self-concept may be considered a 'given'; but I believe there is a huge difference in claiming it as a' victim' vs. 'survivor'. Was I turning to humans or to God? As a believer I have free will and the choice and resulting consequences are mine.

At this point in the healing process, it may be helpful for you to look away from the book, take a deep breath, and honestly test yourself. You cannot change the piece you are currently examining. However, you may have the option to change the effect of the piece but, you only have the capacity to change <u>you...always.</u> So, perhaps it would help you, as it does me today, to take a test as you are holding each piece (past or present) or experiencing a trigger. Is there something you believe you need to claim and/or change to negate the negativity with this piece? If the scenario has current family members still in your life today; perhaps you have the power to delete negativity within you today. You cannot change others, only you. They chose their paths since these past scenarios and you chose yours. Are you, right now, worth working on you to negate any negativity? Are you worth claiming the journey? As a believer, would working on this issue help you be the person God identifies you as being to follow His path? Are you willing to claim it as a possible goal?

RESPONSIBILITY

Personally, I am thankful that I am the only adult I can change. I am thankful the changes in others are not my responsibility, as I oftentimes have a full plate just trying to change me! Within my healing process, responsibility has been key in identification. Struggling to correctly define <u>my</u> responsibility in situations has been extremely important for me in gaining an understanding allowing me to identify my personal goals. Before I define a personal goal, it is mandatory that all requirements for me to meet the goal are my responsibility rather than another person's because I would be placing myself in another's control, in my view, if I did it any other way.

If one accepts such a premise as truth; the assignment of responsibilities throughout the entire healing process is of utmost importance; because, when applied, the whole process is quickened, and by the way, much simpler. Recognizing the proper claiming of responsibilities results in an amazing clarity of seemingly monstrous past situations.

Once I, personally, recognized how important a tool this recognition afforded me, I was able over and over and over to recognize situations in which I had claimed misguided responsibility and had acted on it, many times resulting in misguided guilt. Claiming the responsibility of another as my own is a habit I have labeled, and it is also a habit I choose to stop immediately when I recognize it. I believe proper labeling of the responsibilities in daily living provides one with an excellent insightful tool to use in creating a positive living environment in which to exist. After all, if I am the only adult who I am able to change, why in the world would I choose to claim the responsibility of another; or, on the other hand, why in the world would I choose to give my responsibility of my life to another to control without very careful thought beforehand? After all, I make the choice, I pay the consequence; in the past and in today.

SUPPLEMENT to RESPONSIBILITY

1. Is it important to you that you accept any responsibility required of you?

2. Do you ever transfer your responsibility to another? If so, can you honestly define the action as positive, acceptable, or healthy?

3. Have you accepted another's responsibility as yours?

4. Check all your goals; including ones the ladder-rung you are currently on requires. If you agree that you are the only one you can change and you are the only person in the world that has the exact story contained in your life-story's book, make sure the steps you have assigned yourself for each goal are your responsibility and not another's. Doing so would be a positive.

5. Always note any consistent issue or individual appearing in your story puzzles. If you are required to claim responsibility; you have choices to make. Keeping in mind your responsibility to the others, perhaps by changing your behavior, you will reduce toxicity in your life today. Remember, you pay the consequences for the choices you make.

6. Decide how you are going to celebrate and do it today.

RESPONSIBILITY ADDENDUM

Slipping and sliding in the pit, may have required you to zero in on you alone to hang on and put your foot on the first few rungs of the ladder. I know it did for me and it appeared to be an immeasurable climb to the top. It may be easier for you to see the top of the ladder as the Light seems to become more prominent with each rung. When I was at this point, I do not remember looking down; only up. If you have a like experience as I when crawling off the ladder and <u>standing</u> for the first time to experience life with your new self-identification; you may not be able to explain the experience. Sometimes I secretly wonder if entering Heaven will be akin to finally experiencing the 'new me' excited for the next chapter's responsibilities in my life.

The ability to stand will allow you to be on the Foundation in the Light with the readiness to experience the Gospel of Peace the Bible describes as you stand up and slide your feet into the shoes provided with God's armor to protect against Satan. You may find it worthwhile to be considering definitions within your ladder goals that may pertain to the Foundation on which you will be standing. When you crawl off the ladder, surrounded in the Light, you will no longer be standing on a ladder rung. Do you agree that you may define the 'Foundation' on which you are standing differently than the 'foundation' on which you existed prior to the ladder experience? If you already are feeling like a 'new' person, could you also agree to the possibility that you have been working to define your upcoming 'Foundation'? Can you also agree that God has been helping you to gain the ability to use new capabilities in responsibilities to follow His leading?

Prior to the ladder experience, I do not think I was much of a problem for Satan. I do not remember ever spending a lot of time turning to God for direction initially. For me, personally, it was on the upper rungs of the ladder where I began realizing the power of the Light's guidance. I was also, therefore, recognizing the power I personally, was experiencing. The definition of 'power' with respect to my daily life includes the strength or manner with which I have the capacity to combat past negativity. Negativity that prevented me from being the 'new' person I am today. If you agree with this thinking, and you are beginning to feel like the 'new' person; it might be helpful for you to identify the most destructive negative you have recognized on the ladder. What have your goals and the changes you have made in the goals taught you about your biggest 'stumbling block'? For me, it was a self-definition of me: lack of worth and non-equal. Yesterday, as I was typing this section, I got up and set the computer open on the chair to step outside and stretch a few minutes. When I returned, my dog was standing on the computer keyboard looking at me. I immediately yelled at Satan because I believe he would much rather I lean into my computer-illiterate self-concept and not finish this project, than to turn to God and continue. I recognize in this day, that the 'strength' I began using in becoming the 'new' me while on the ladder, allowed me to feel more and more worthy and equal. If your history is one of abuse, you may say the same. As I am now trying to follow HIS guidance, I have recognized that it is these same destructive negatives I fought on the ladder that I now sense as stumbling blocks on the path following God's leading to trip me. And I now describe this new finding as spiritual warfare and the 'past negative issue of my self-concept' the place where the devil dipped his spear before sending it at me. That definition is helpful in quickly negating the negative and polishing the positive by simply 'instructing' the devil to turn and run'.

I am responsible for choices I made on the ladder as well as paths I choose to follow when off the ladder. You will also be responsible for those choices and live with the consequences of the choices you make. We all have responsibilities in this world no matter what choice we make. However, do not the choices we make also impact the responsibilities we will be assigned?

Spiritual warfare is not a subject that I had spent time thinking about until just recently in my life. I now recognize ways in which it was affecting my ladder experience also. I will share some recent insights I've identified for you to possibly consider. Each of us has experienced situations in our lives that may be unique to us within any scenario in our puzzle. This is a huge advantage I have labeled as a God 'gets me' and I think is providing me with insights. One is that spiritual warfare will be an ongoing issue as any believer strives to follow God's directions. However, you have the gifts available to battle the enemy. I don't know about you; but I'm thankful that all I am required to do is to face Satan and yell at him, even if it is silently. I know from experience, it works! It also worked on the ladder before I could stand to face him and yell. The positive result can be defined as peace overcoming negative anguish.

My guess is that you are working hard on your healing because HE has an important job that only you have the requirements to accomplish for HIM. If not, He would be assigning the job to another. You can do it because HE picked you and will be with you every step of the way. You obviously have what is required to fulfill the responsibilities. Over and over God has shown me that HE has a path for me to take and, if I desire to follow HIS will, amazing results can be accomplished. It is interesting to note, however; that whenever I feel discouraged doing so and begin to question; I can generally identify my reaction to negativity connected to what I fought the hardest on the ladder experience (for me--I am equal to you/I have worth as a human being). I suggest, if this makes sense to you, that you label your biggest threat to control in the 'new' you that you are becoming. Because, Satan would much rather have you believing the negative; he needs soldiers. For as long as you have God right beside you as your main Ally, you are surely not making the devil a happy camper! I believe any and every believer on the healing ladder is a threat to the devil.

Consequently, I believe every believer on the healing ladder is involved in spiritual warfare. I believe each believer on the healing ladder has God right there with him/her offering HIS peace. And

I also believe any and every believer has a job with responsibilities waiting for them to follow when sliding into the shoes provided for the walk along God's chosen path on the Foundation. Psalm 119:105 gives definitions for what God provides: *"Your word is a lamp for my feet, a light on my path."* (NIV p669). I am not to do your job, neither is anyone else; God has chosen you. He has given you the strength, power, and armor needed for the job. You are the one who He's chosen for the task and He is with you now on every ladder rung. If you lean into the negativity, like I still label myself as doing at times today, by questioning your abilities to fulfill responsibilities, how is that not questioning God and His ability? You have already been dealing with your threats. You are much higher right now on the ladder than you were before you identified the negativities. You are already capable of negating the negative and polishing the positive. You will be able to take on the responsibilities because you can choose to have HIM guide your each and every step. You are already using the armor. He desires to be your chosen Ally. He has gifted us with much; some of which we have not yet experienced.

INNER ROOM

When trying to describe the healing process, I have found this simile to be appropriate: What if it is as though we each have deep within us a room with at least one item labeled 'secrets' and it is to this room we go to peel our layers when hurting or fighting to clearly understand a situation in which we find ourselves.

My room contains a door with a handle and a lock. It also contains a light switch. I believe one of the scariest things in being an adult (tall child?) is that I now have total responsibility regarding my room. This room is only within me containing my quirks and uniqueness and secrets. I am now tall enough to unlock the door and strong enough to open the door. I am also now tall enough to choose to leave the door shut and perhaps also locked; the choice is completely mine because I am now tall enough to open the door and to turn on the light. I now may start peeling honestly; or consciously choose to go into the room, leave it dark, weep and wail, refusing to claim or to accept any responsibility under any circumstances. I may even be tall enough at this point in my life, to choose to remove the light from its socket! I am also tall enough to consciously choose to ignore the room completely by not approaching it.

However, because I am tall, and have responsibilities and a job, I am no longer called a child; therefore, am I not now required to accept certain responsibilities to God? And, in addition to that requirement, am I not also now required to accept certain responsibilities to all others within my environment? Because I am a responsible adult, do I not have responsibility to claim what I am being shown in this healing process?

Is it possible that many of the experiences we have in our lives, as adults, contain lessons to teach us how to walk closer with God? And, if so; is it then possible that, if we choose to not make such examinations by ignoring the inner room altogether, we will be given more opportunities to identify the lessons we need to learn?

SUPPLEMENT to INNER ROOM

1. Although it is not uncommon for me to talk to others regarding problematic situations revealed in puzzles; I believe that my healing process is my personal struggle as their healing process is to them. And, although certain individuals represent frequent pieces in both past and present toxic puzzles I examine in my book, my personal struggle remains mine alone. Consequently, there were many times, particularly in the first few years of my struggle, where I chose to simply collapse, weep and wail. I have learned that I am a valuable enough person that a few tears spent here and there for me were not a sin. Sometimes, now while living in the Light, something happens, and I feel the need for another pity party. However, in the past few years, I have set the timer for 5-10 minutes; it may happen twice a year, depending on the triggers. I am the only one invited to these parties and if weeping and wailing is expected, I schedule the party when no one else will be interrupted by any noise I make. In my opinion, you are deserving of doing the same. I believe sometimes we all have negatives come into our lives which may present an excellent time for a short-lived private pity party.

2. Are you discovering any responsibilities you should have claimed that you did not in your puzzles? If so, are you still not claiming your responsibilities; and, if so, have you decided to change? If so, have you set the goal with concrete steps written to prove to you that you have accomplished each one?

3. If you believe you have already identified tools you feel are helpful to you in your healing process because you have chosen to try them, you have another cause for celebration; even if it

is going outside tonight and looking at the galaxies, assuming you are lucky enough to be able to have the choice to see the stars at night!

4. If you believe you have responsibilities to God, have you identified and claimed them?

INNER-ROOM ADDENDUM

My Inner Room is where I am today when examining me and questioning me honestly. Honesty is a requirement for my self-evaluations. Am I doing what I say I am doing? Am I using the strength I began feeling on the ladder properly? Are my actions and thoughts reflecting what I say I believe? Am I loving as God directs? Do I act according to His definitions of me? Do I have goals for the present day? Are they different because I am a different person? Am I not a victim, but a survivor? Am I allowing a present-day trigger to victimize me? I have strength available to apply the tools I was unable to use when I started the ladder climb. Today I am not on the ladder. I have the availability of the armor whenever it is needed... and God is my Ally! My goal to follow God's path for me requires yelling at the devil quite frequently. Consequently, when examining me, I often feel the Breastplate of Righteousness offers topics to examine.

I go to my inner room to pray when personal questions come to mind and I feel as though I am dealing with spiritual warfare. When I sense I am standing on a battlefield, the armor of God comes to my mind and sometimes I am not certain I am correctly defining the steps I am to take. Obviously, as a believer desiring to follow God's path for me to walk, I desire to also define and claim the responsibilities He assigns me on that path correctly. It is important that I 'am right' and in line with what He is assigning for me to accomplish for Him. If you can relate to this experience, then you too probably experience the following: Questions I deal with at these times are asking what is required to be right with God? Sometimes I think these questions are appropriate: God, why is this happening to me right now? ... What is it that you want me to learn from this that is a requirement for me to do the job you are preparing me for on this path? It has been these questions that often will be answered with a surprising insight to a previously unanswered question experienced on early ladder rungs. It may have produced a negative at that time.

However now it is turning to a positive that requires some polishing in the present. I define the experience as a gift to me that this piece of the armor provides showing me that the choices, I am making at this moment, are 'right with God'.

If you agree with my statements that abuse <u>always</u> teaches the victim that he/she is deserving of the abuse, not equal, blah blah; then you will probably agree it is difficult for that victim to easily accept that he/she is 'right with God'. Consequently, another gift God provides believers which helps me with this issue is His many positive descriptions of believers...I am at the point today at which I can much more readily accept that, if I follow HIS definitions of me, I can define myself as being 'right with God' as I walk the path following His lead.

It is at this point that I am going to share with you the insight, confirmation, and encouragement that surprised me in a Bible-study class I attended recently. It is nearly impossible for me to attend church often and not hear about a man named Paul. After all, he wrote more books in the Bible than anyone else. He is quoted often. He was a highly educated man and met with leaders of the world in his lifetime. Obviously, I have recognized for years that he was to be recognized and studied. I knew he had an unidentified ailment that God refused to heal. I also knew that he was a tentmaker when he needed income for his travels, which made sense to me, as I assumed people no doubt required tents in that day. But it was in the class, while the attendees were conversing about the tentmaking, when it hit me that God had used Paul's life speak to people like me. At times in my life today, I still fight to feel equal to you. Guess what I learned in that class about tentmaking...it was a filthy, dirty, and stench-producing job! (I raised my hand in class and asked this question for verification: "So, I would certainly never have asked Paul to come over at break to share a cup of tea with us?"...the response was laughter.)

God could have had this man be a leader of a country rather than a tent maker. After all, Paul met with leaders of countries. His name is on many pages in my Bible in the New Testament as well as mentioned in sermons and classes in the church I attend today while other men in the Bible are referenced as being with Paul. It is Paul who God often chooses to speak to you and me in the Bible. But God had him 'smelling yucky' when working on the tents probably causing people to walk far away from him. Does it remind you of a Man named Jesus who was born in an animal's stable, then a carpenter, and then going into homes of people where others would not tread, into tents, and sleep in fields? I am thankful God says that I am good enough for Him to love and perhaps do a job for Him; even when He knows each of my puzzle pieces better than I. I believe God understands me; and, if He 'gets me', then I am certain that He 'gets you' also. He gave Paul the smelly job of making tents...I guess this all means that God chose Paul to 'get me' also .... wow! This is very encouraging to me when I am honestly contemplating my shortcomings privately in my inner room. I find it more encouraging than turning to humans who may not define me as God does.

In his letter to the church in Corinth Paul states in I Corinthians 1:27-30 how God chooses for His will to be accomplished: *"God chose the foolish things of the world to shame the wise; God chose the weak things of the world to shame the strong. God chose the lowly things of this world and the despised things--and the things that are not--to nullify the things that are, so that no one may boast before him. It is because of him that you are in Christ Jesus, who has become for us wisdom from God--that is our righteousness, holiness and redemption."* (NIV p1238). If you have an issue with still being triggered to lean into a low self-concept when striving to follow God's leading, thinking about this passage while in your inner-room contemplating might help encourage you, also.

And, in I Corinthians 2:4-5, Paul references the above verse: *"My message and my preaching were not with wise and persuasive words, but with a demonstration of the Spirit's power, so that your faith might not rest on human wisdom, but on God's power."* (NIV p1238) My opinion is that God's gift of the Holy Spirit's indwelling of me when

I accepted Him and became a believer tells me that I do not have to be concerned about my bucket full of shortcomings. He has me protected and covered and, if I follow HIM instead of my opinions of the purpose, the job will be done and done the way that is 'right' with HIM. I believe that a reason you are reading this page right at this moment could be because God has chosen you and has a path for you to follow...only you can do it. Believers have been gifted with the Breastplate of Righteousness.

THE LIGHT

Within a short time in the pit, I decided I did <u>not</u> want to stay! The more success I recognized in my climb, the more the Light became concrete to me. The Light brought clarity. Light is helpful when one is examining anything. When engaged in my healing process, I am usually working in my life story and examining past situations. I choose situations to examine that I define as problematic; then I try to decide why I believe there is a problem within the situation. Each time I identify an answer (define a puzzle piece), I feel as though light has been added to make the situation become clear.

Some of us may have experienced a camp setting requiring one to walk on a path from the sleeping cabin to the main hall at night, alone. Hearing a sound ahead may bring a feeling of panic until a flashlight is turned on by another camper joining you. Suddenly, the walk is not as frightening with a flashlight and a friend. Everything has now been identified and you feel safe because it is now familiar and is helping it make sense to you. Sometimes, the healing process feels much the same as the unfamiliar paths in the dark woods!

Because I now experience living in the Light with a clearer understanding and have been identifying much of the unknown, I am able to make healthier choices for me. Before I started climbing the healing ladder, I did not make healthy choices for me. Choosing to stay on the healing ladder and finding the puzzle pieces that were missing allowed me to gain insight to the big picture. The more pieces I had, the clearer the bigger picture became as I began to see how all the little pieces were fitting. It is much the same as when working a jigsaw puzzle. Once I realize the pieces in my hand do not fit into the big picture in the way I had anticipated, and I change my mind, picking up other colored pieces, the latter choice brings more pleasing results for me. I had to choose to make a change.

The Light provides me with courage. With each success and celebration on the healing ladder, came a bit of courage. I may not have recognized it each time, but I <u>did</u> recognize that it was becoming easier to say words such as 'no'; as well as change the way I dealt with certain ongoing situations.

These days, I feel as though my past life story is in a closed book on a shelf because I am living in the Light. Sometimes I choose to take it down to remind me of certain situations I have examined. In trying to offer ideas that may help you, I am choosing to open it much more often than normal. But, before I felt I was living <u>in</u> the Light, the book was always open because I felt as though I was trapped in my life story.

Perhaps one of the biggest benefits for me in living in the Light is that, instead of being trapped in my life story, I have come to realize that my life story defines who I am today. And I have much for which to be thankful, <u>including</u> much of the portions in which the reasons for my climbing the healing ladder are located.

Now, I know I need to explain what I have just stated!!! I truly hope you have already read something you have felt may be of some help to you. If so, know this...I am writing this book because I climbed the healing ladder. I climbed the healing ladder because I was totally broken to the point of lying on the floor and pulling the cord of the phone to the floor to call a friend. I could not stand; I was broken to the point of not remembering when I last ate. If I had not been in that place, I most certainly never would be writing something like this. If it helps you, I am thankful. I would not be as aware of living in the Light, had I not experienced being so broken.

I am thankful for my life story. The healing process has taught me that my life story contributes to who I am and what I am. The

Light is an incredibly good thing. In my personal story, when I am aware of the Light, I am aware of the presence of God. I am thankful to Him for providing me the Light in which I have access to His offerings such as clarity, identification, armor, courage, strength, companionship, and the leadership I need to be where I am today in my life story providing the ability to live pages that will, for the most part, make me smile when I thumb through this layer of my story years from now.

My relationship with God is totally different than any other of my life. I know He is with me when I cannot see Him and cannot hear His voice. He is often referred to as 'Heavenly Father' and believers referenced as 'a child of God' which are probably the best descriptions I can offer because when I am broken, I am not a grown up, tall, capable adult; but, rather a small, quite helpless, unknowing, confused child who definitely needs His guidance. As a child, if we had a father, we each needed his guidance. However, a surprising number have been raised by fathers who were not welcomed but, rather, feared.

I would like to take this opportunity to try to explain how this special relationship with God has been so helpful to me, specifically on the healing ladder. Please afford me the opportunity in this section to be who I am when it is He and I. I would like to slip into a genre perhaps more fitting to me with God when on my healing ladder.

And, by the way, if you are one who believes that all smart adults know what we are saying when we say things like "God told me" or "God wants me to____", you are wrong! It is only the brave ones of us who ask. People who have asked me what I mean when I make like statements are not stupid adults, but, rather, brave people determined to learn. I admire their courage because I have only had the courage to ask questions about God to others who talk about Him in recent years. But when people ask me, they often also say: "I have never understood what people mean when they say those things". I did not understand either.........I do now.

Perhaps the healing-ladder experience was required of me before I could understand why people said things like: "God showed me" or "God said". I think it works kind of like this...as I grew from a little child, lots of other things got bigger too. Like, maybe instead of pennies, I got nickels, then dimes, then quarters. And the words in the books I read got bigger, especially books required in college. A dictionary was my constant companion in college. I did not want college to be as hard as grade-school and some high-school classes had been. The words I studied and could use got bigger. And then I could talk about things without seeing them in front of me; but the problem is that if somebody is talking about something that I have never seen nor heard nor touched nor known about before and is using big unfamiliar words, I still have trouble 'getting it'. This is when I think I would pretend I got it and just be quiet so others would not call me dumb and stupid. Sometimes a problem with we big people is, we like to use the big words. But, when we feel uncomfortable with others, some of us still pretend we are something or someone different than who we really are. Sometimes some people start using the same big words but, they cannot explain the words they are using!

When talking about God, many people use three big words a lot. Each of the words start with 'OMNI' probably because they all are used to describe God. 'omni' means 'all' but, I think, even bigger; like not just everything on your plate but all the food on the table or in the house or whole universe or even bigger than the biggest we know about! So, I think that is the reason the three words start with 'omni', because they are all used to describe God. I often would get two of them mixed up. I kept it a secret from other big people, so please do not give my secret away, ok? It took me a long time to really 'get it' myself, so I will just talk about the words in my own secret way here for a little while...in the same language I use when I am talking to God when no one else can hear my prayer. I am comfortable talking to God because I never feel I need to pretend because He 'gets me' and still loves me and NEVER makes me feel stupid; but always helps me feel better about myself.

The first word is **OMNIPRESENT** ---This is the easiest word because I understood the word 'present'. At school if somebody is not there, they are absent and if they are there, they are present...that is what 'present' means, I think, when Christians talk about God. (But, to me, the other kind of 'present' is like God too; because I think having God with me in my life is better than the best present any human could ever give me.) I guess I will have to get brave enough one day to ask a Christian teacher if they mean this kind of present too; are you brave enough to ask?

So, if you asked me to explain, I could say God is a great present I wanted in my life and He is all over (present) in every place at the same time! He is with you at the same time He is with me where I am, even if I am in a pit in the ground; because He is everywhere, all over, every second of every day! ... pretty neat, huh?

And I know He is present even if I cannot see Him because when I am scared, if I just start talking to Him, I start to feel safer and safer...that is how I know He is with me even though I can never see Him, and I cannot hear what His voice sounds like. He does not need to talk to me, for me to know He is with me. At night, I am glad that I do not have to see Him nor hear Him to know He is there because I can feel safe to go to sleep because I want to close my eyes.

OMNISCIENT is another one of the three big words. The part of the word after the 'OMNI' sort of looks like the word science. I think science is hard to understand which helps me remember that this word means God 'gets it'. He understands everything. I am glad He gets it all because there are a lot of people who do not understand me; they just don't get it! But guess what...God does. He understands me better than I do and when I ask Him about stuff about me that I stay confused about, He is smart enough to figure out a way to show me the answers. Even when I cannot see nor hear Him, He knows how He can help me understand something when the people I can see and hear cannot help me understand. Do you ever get angry or sad and do not understand when something happens to you? I do. And then, after a while, like days or maybe the next month or year, I understand it. Maybe, after a long time later, I find out it was ok… or, maybe even a good thing. I think, maybe, God explains stuff to me that way sometimes. People cannot help me get it like God can.

I am glad I was smart enough to tell Him I wanted Him to be with me in my life because now, He is always there to help me get smart enough to understand a whole bunch of stuff. Even like why I am sad or scared or why something bad happened to me. Sometimes it takes me a long time to understand it; probably because I generally require Him to show me a lot of different ways to see the answer. And sometimes I think the answer maybe has a lot of parts and steps I am required to learn and understand before I can finally get the answers and understand why. It is sort of like when I was smaller and had to learn to add and subtract before I could learn how to multiply and divide. That took a long time too.

There are some things in my brain that I wish were not there! So maybe because God knows everything and understands all about everything He knows; and He knows me better than I do, He has decided that I would not be as happy as I am today if He answers every question that I am asking Him. Have you ever wondered about something but had a funny feeling that maybe you did not want to know? Sometimes, when I get that feeling, I think maybe I am not supposed to to know that answer; so maybe I will stop fighting to find out. Then I start feeling better and sometimes start doing something fun instead. If I feel a lot better when I quit trying to figure out the answer about something that happened before, and then feel a lot better about today after I quit; I will decide maybe I feel those good feelings because God is showing me to <u>not</u> try to figure that part out because it already happened, and I cannot change what has already happened. But I think God sometimes lets me choose what kind of day I will have today; and sometimes He chooses.

Because God knows everything, He knows and understands what is going to happen in my future and I do not. So, I am happier when I do not try to understand stuff about my future, especially when other people are mixed up in the part I am wondering about. It can be exciting sometimes to say to God that I am curious to see how something will turn out in the end. I have told people that I would never write a book...well, you can see how that turned out!

OMNIPOTENT means the strongest of anything or anyone anyplace. It is like anybody or anything that decides to fight God is going to lose and they are going to lose when and how God says they are going to lose! Maybe you have never been so scared you were afraid to close your eyes or maybe afraid to open them. Maybe you have never been in a place where you could not move or have a drink of water or ask anyone for help.

But someone who has been in those places totally understands how important it would be to know that there is One Who knows what is happening and Who is there with him/her. Jesus was experiencing the same thing when He was nailed to the cross, so Jesus knows AND understands hurting and scared people.

Now, here is the thing that helps people who are on the healing ladder dealing with this type of issue: If God is the one who made the earth and sky and is the strongest of all and He is with these people (the one who cannot move and the person who will not let the other move); then the person who is doing the hurting must not believe in God. The Bible says people who do those things to children make God angry.

If I did something that made God angry enough to come after me, I think I would be more scared than I have been of anything else in my whole life!

And guess what, I believe all these three words about my Heavenly Father. And I believe He is angry with anyone who hurts one of His children and I believe I am one of His children and have always been one of His children and will always be one of His children just like I am today. So, because He is always with me and all three of these words tell what He is like, it is o.k. that I am not the strongest nor the smartest; because He knows me and all about everything I do and everything that happens to me... before... and now... and forever... even after I die!

The Bible is about God and has in it many of the words He said. It talks about Him wanting to take care of the bad stuff, I do not have to think about that. It helps me not to be afraid of the bad stuff that happens when I think about Him being omnipotent and omniscient and omnipresent because that means that He is stronger, and He knows and understands all about my whole life story (even the part that has not happened yet) and He is always with me if I want Him to be.

The environment in which I live offers me the option of being in light. Outside, in the daytime, it is light outside; but I can choose to close my eyes and not accept the light or go inside and cover all the windows to not be in light. At night, when it is dark outside, I can choose to stay in the dark or turn on a light outside or go inside and turn on lights (or, maybe I choose to not turn on the light and stay in the dark inside).

The Light that I talk about in this book is different from the light we turn on and off and I cannot turn It off. But we all have choices about this Light. I believe the Light I am talking about in this book comes from God. I believe It keeps me always with Him because He put me in the middle of It when I asked Him to be with me.

I think maybe, when I am in Heaven and try to walk up to God, the Light will be strong... but not a scary strong; it will be a good strong, I think. The closer I go to God, the safer I feel because the Light is all around me and so It is protecting me and helping me. I feel His presence by just thinking about Him. I never have to be afraid of being alone in a scary place. If I get really scared fast, it is hard for me to remember He is with me because I cannot see Him there. But if I try to remember and talk to Him, not out loud because I want to be quiet, but with my thinking voice instead of my talking voice; He listens very carefully. I know He does because every time I talk to Him when I am scared, I begin to feel safer. I try to remember not to be afraid of the bad stuff because when I die, I think it will be even easier than it is now to know for sure I am with Him and I will be excited because it will be forever and ever, and the bad stuff will not be in Heaven… just the good stuff and the safe people.

SUPPLEMENT to THE LIGHT

If you agree with me as to the definition of the Light in your healing process, allow me to add that I strongly suggest frequent praying at each step of the healing process you choose to take. Remember, He will be listening if you talk out loud or silently.

OMNIPRESENT   OMNISCIENT   OMNIPOTENT

THE LIGHT ADDENDUM

Fellow Believer,

I suggest that you consider writing "The Light Addendum" here and dating it; enabling you to easily recognize your growth to this date and allowing you possible reasons for celebration often in times to follow.

The following chapters involve issues that were oftentimes present within each stack of puzzle pieces I attacked within my healing process. Perhaps you may sense some familiarity with one or more of them. I assume you will also find recurring issues as you go through your examinations of various situations within your life story, particularly when recurring individuals are characters within the various scenarios. So, adjust and tweak using whatever is applicable to your story, feeling free to substitute my concept labels to those more applicable to your life story.

My experience is that, as new situations arise, or I examine new puzzles, the process remains applicable and beneficial.

VICTIM/ ENABLER/ HELPER?

I do not know about you; but in my mind, the word 'victim' brings forth the thought of a negative situation in which the victim believes he/she has no control of his/her life and the availability of escape is nonexistent. Negative experiences can create lasting effects that may disrupt one's life forever if not addressed. I believe that anyone who has been in such a scenario would benefit from a healing process in which he/she is respected by others, as the process can be difficult. The time the process takes is dependent upon choices made but supportive and respectful available people may shorten the time required of one who chooses to experience the healing process. Although time spent in the healing process may be longer if the victim does not have a group of supporters, I would encourage anyone who is hurting and feeling as though he/she is broken, to begin the process. Personally, I would NEVER wish to return to the life I had prior to my healing experience.

In sharing my healing process within the pages of this book, my intent was to only talk about adults on the healing ladder; however, I feel the need to sneak a warning into this paragraph regarding children who have been victimized. I believe caring adults easily have the potential to be enablers, especially with children who have been victimized. When someone, particularly a child, has experienced unacceptable situations in his/her life; it is natural, in my opinion, for others to pity him/her. Is it possible that, if we allow ourselves to act without thought for a length of time, we might assume the role of an enabler rather than helper in a desire to 'fix it'? Is it wise, in such a situation to take time to question what your actions are teaching a 'child victim'? If, in fact, your goal is to be a helper; is it possible that the child has not been taught the life skills necessary for one to be successfully independent in life when the current caring people are no longer available? These children may have difficulty in learning life skills such as reading and math. However, are we truly helping if we are ignoring this possibility and just giving or buying things to and for them? I believe, when working with a child from a victim situation, it is the responsibility of the adult to consistently examine not only what the child is being taught with each action, but how it will aid the child in becoming as independent as possible in his/her adult life. Could your actions be teaching the child much more than how to read or find the correct answer to the math problem? Does the child have personal goals for his/her life? What about after this earthly life?

I believe there is a fine line between enabling and helping. My definition of an 'enabler' is a person who, in some way, supports the 'victim' to remain in the dark side of the healing ladder. I think that, in many ways, to <u>not</u> be an enabler with a significant other is difficult, both/either adult or child. As caring people, we have a desire to help. We want the hurt to heal and the victim to be a happy person. If the victim is someone we love; when they hurt, we hurt... we want to fix it, and right now!

It can also be extremely difficult, particularly when a loved one is hurting, to take care of self. Therefore, monitoring if one is sacrificing self- respect, and/or accepting unhealthy responsibilities, and/or ignoring other duties to self or to others may be required. However, I believe there are times in which adults may be placed in situations in which, for a given time at least, personal sacrifices are not only our responsibility, but a necessity. A situation which, of course, makes the decisions not only emotional but much more difficult to identify clearly.

Is it possible, however, that an adult would <u>choose</u> to take on the role of a 'victim'? Could it also be possible that a 'self-chosen victim' has the potential to pull another into the darkness with him/her? When in the helper role, would monitoring self not be a wise step to consider? Particularly if one is debating the conscious choices of the 'victim'; or, if the scenario remains constant over a period of months or years? Would it be possible for an enabler/helper to forfeit his/her responsibilities to others and, possibly, even oneself in such circumstances? Is a proper term for identification of one choosing to live the 'victim facade': 'victim' or 'controller'?

However, in looking back and examining my healing process, I noted an early issue about myself. When I suddenly found myself in the pit and beginning the climb on the healing ladder, I was extremely demanding and 'over-the-top' egotistical. I screamed at God that I could not feel His presence. The friend I would frequently call, probably rambling until early morning, was required to leave for her job around 5:00 am! She sacrificed a night's sleep listening to me. As in my case, it might be necessary to begin the climb on the healing ladder and experience a distance from the pit before one realizes that it may not be convenient for another to listen to ramblings in the wee hours of the morning. Or to also realize, how much time and energy is being spent in 'pity parties'; and to become frustrated with the weeping and wailing. A gift the healing-ladder process provides one is the choice to do something about the situation he/she is in today.

I defy anyone to listen to an abuse situation being described and conclude it was a positive, encouraging experience. I recognize that some stories require an initial time of 'self-centeredness'. However, it is my experience that 'looking beyond self' will shorten the healing time. Each time I looked beyond me in examining a puzzle piece, I believe my time on the ladder shortened. The anger and poor self-descriptions dissipate, and recognition of inner strength grows. Then, the result becomes more readily recognized with referring to self as a survivor rather than a victim, as a victim has little to no strength nor control.

I began the conscious work to heal and to change the current day's picture of my life story. My friend could not do the work, only I could examine situations to find the correct puzzle pieces which became easier with each ladder rung I climbed. I sincerely must question if I could be writing this today had I not experienced friends in my environment, at each step on the ladder, willing to accept the role of helper. Today, I remain thankful for such friends just a phone call away. On this day, however, I like to believe it is a mutual availability between us; hopefully, they would agree. It has been my life story and the help provided from friends, as much as any other tool, that has allowed me to define a helper as I do today.

Helpers realize that my life story is mine. Consequently, they provide me with safety in sharing. Unless I ask, they do not provide advice; but rather they ask penetrating questions that make me think, questions such as: Have you thought about...What do you see in the picture .... What do you think is the significance of...Do you think it would help you if you_____?". In questioning in this format, they are giving me the respect of recognition that I am the one responsible for today's page in my life story. Their questions exhibit their excellent listening skills. They have the capacity to hear the important clues in my sharing that point to the puzzle pieces I should be examining but am not locating. And it is because they have listened to my story.

In my opinion, an effective listening tool for a helper to use is the ability to wait for the individual's immediate response to a penetrating question. Sometimes such an immediate answer indicates the response comes 'right from the gut'. Oftentimes the individual does not realize what he/she had just said. I think the more surprised he/she is at what you repeat back, the more important the information is to his/her identification process. Therefore, by repeating words back to the individual, the helper may ask if he/she thinks it may be helpful to examine, in the privacy of the inner room, why he/she may have said those particular words. By doing so, the helper may aid the individual to discover a key to assist him/her in finding an important piece to his/her puzzle.

In my personal counseling sessions, I became aware of an inability to recall portions of the visit. I decided a prerequisite for me to see a given counselor would be receiving permission to tape the session. By listening to the tapes, I was able to note my 'comments from the gut'. I not only gained new information about myself I had not previously recognized, but also a few unexpected surprises.

Helpers realize that if I am calling for help, I am asking for help rather than judgement. They recognize that I am already doing an excellent job of self-judging if I am calling for help. If I were sure of myself, I would not be requesting help today. No matter how intense I become; they allow me to lean into my current emotions by remaining low-key yet concrete by a word, or possibly a touch on the hand. However, they are respectful of my personal, both physically and psychologically, at all times. They are <u>always</u> honest with me.

The role of helper is, in my mind, one of the most important gifts we are given. To be able to be of an aid to another who is hurting and broken can be life changing, to the broken and/or to the helper. For me personally, when 'the rug was pulled out from under me suddenly'; the definition of a friend and an aunt, already important to me and in my environment, changed to a definition of helpers who assisted me to move into a whole new lifestyle required of me before I could climb the ladder effectively. I could not feel God's presence, so, my guess is that He provided the concrete that I desperately needed by offering a trusted friend working alongside me weekly and a loving aunt living nearby as available supporters. I can only trust that He also provided them the sense of rest they, no doubt desperately needed at that time.

My personal belief is that significant others, in the role of helpers, have been available to me on each rung of the healing ladder as well as in the freedom the Light offers; because they are the concrete God recognizes I need in my life to keep me walking on solid ground. When I sense the ground beneath me is not the Solid Rock, I ask for help. I trust my friends realize that I am expecting the same from them. Is it possible that mutual responsibilities and respect accorded each adult within one's environment must be recognized by all parties involved for all to exist in the positive rather than in the negative? My experiences with significant others who have taken the role of helper in my life have taught me that the answer to the last question for me is yes .... absolutely, yes. I believe that I say this today because I am not identifying myself with the term 'victim' neither do I refer to the others as 'victim'; but each assured the other is available desiring to respectfully listen.

Some may believe being a victim has its perks, however. Thinking about a scenario including a victim, I note that the victim is getting all the attention. A victim may interrupt a meeting. A victim may stop traffic. A victim may pull people out of their homes or offices. A victim may be watched on television by countless others. A victim is not expected to accept the same responsibilities as others within the environment. The onlookers' sensitivities are not usually toward the helpers; but, rather, toward the victim in the situation. Others may sacrifice personal responsibilities when assisting victims. The victim is not expected to take responsibility; but, rather only to receive aid from others.

Do we not, in fact, assign the expected responsibilities of a victim to others; or readily take them onto ourselves? Is it possible for one to consciously choose to live a facade as a victim or to remain in the darkness of a victim's existence to avoid responsibilities or, possibly, to gain perceived needed attention from others in one's environment? However, if one chooses to play a facade role as a victim, is he/she consciously choosing not to stand? Is he/she expecting others to take responsibility to carry him/her? If one chooses to play a facade role as a victim, is he/she being respectful in any way to those around him/her?

Other scenarios are also possible. Is it possible that some may take advantage of another they define as victim? Is it possible that one choosing to live the facade of a victim may be victimizing others? Is it possible, therefore, that a helper may be allowing another to victimize him/her, perhaps unconsciously?

Whenever the concept of victim is within a given situation one is examining in the healing process, would not proper identification of the <u>entire</u> situation be a prerequisite not to be ignored? Within the world of adults, you are the only adult you will be able to change. Your choice, your personal consequences. Does not each of the individuals have certain rights and responsibilities within his/her abilities?

I think the society in which I live practices a belief, however unconscious it may be, that familial situations are perceived differently than all others. If a person has been victimized by a neighbor, would any of us encourage the individual to keep in touch or to visit or to attend any services honoring the perpetrator? But what if the perpetrator is a family member? Is it possible that all of us accept the belief that rules change, if family members are involved, without realizing the possible affect it may have on a victim, or on a support person...Why?

Could it be possible that the victim is dealing with the same belief system described, consciously or unconsciously? The acceptance of a responsibility to one's perpetrator may present misguided or even self-inflicted toxicity. Does he/she feel because the perpetrator is family.... So, must it then be accepted as fact that a 'familial perpetrator' should be granted 'rights', particularly by the victim, that other perpetrators would not be allowed within the scenario...Why?

Would it be possible that I, as a helper, encourage this victim to keep in touch with a perpetrator ... after all, he/she is family? Would this definition of support be toxic for this victim, or helpful? ... Why? How important would it be, as a support to this victim/survivor to continually keep such a question in mind? How important is it for us to all remember, whichever role we are in, that my life story is mine alone and your life story is yours alone? We each will pay our individual consequences for our individual choices made this day.

The healthiest choices I have felt required to make generally resulted in consequences that were not the easiest to experience, probably because they often involved significant others. However, the most difficult decisions may bring forth the most powerful results, although time may be required to recognize and label the positives. When I called myself a victim, I felt weak and extremely vulnerable; not capable of making choices. When I began calling myself survivor, I was feeling stronger and wiser. The hardest, scariest decisions have brought forth the more pleasant days in addition to the most concrete awareness of my Savior's presence.

I am thankful that, on this day, I can state I am a survivor and not a victim. What follows is a comparison of the definitions I give to the words provided from my experience on my personal healing-ladder climb:

VICTIM	SURVIVOR
in the dark side non-entity/ unworthy deserving of the worst	see self as equal to others (nearly always)
overwhelming/ crippling fear and/or anger	sometimes a sense of sadness around it/ sometimes recognizable short-lived anger/ most often, no recognizable emotion
helpless child/ void of control	using adult skills
totally self-absorbed and self-centered	ability to see/ act beyond and outside self
afraid to try for fear of falling down into the pit or committing suicide	willingness to experiment with suggestions of others/ recognizing ability to choose to adjust or reject

I am totally unlovable.	If God loves equally, then He loves me as much as He loves you and I have the strength to declare same.
To be an obedient Christian, I am required to forgive whatever the cost is to me.	Forgiveness does not hold the threat it once did; however, I do not accept an inclusion of denying one's essence within my definition.
I am too weak to fight for equality to others in my environment.	I know I have the strength to fight for equality to others within my environment.
I suffer nightmares when I try to sleep at night.	I may have a nightmare as a result of a trigger once in a fifteen-year period.
The abuse is still consuming me. When awake, it is only with much difficulty I can concentrate to any degree on anything else.	I am able to close my life-story book and put it on the shelf to open it at will. When I choose to close it, I am immediately able to turn and focus easily on another topic or project.
Negative triggers interrupt whatever I am doing.	Most often I am able to identify and/or prevent triggers from disturbing daily activities.

SUPPLEMENT to VICTIM/ ENABLER/ HELPER?

1. Think about the people who know you best; perhaps know more about your life story than others. There have been times when friends who have met people in my past-layer puzzles are the most helpful. However, list as many people as possible for support, as it is not reasonable to always turn to one individual.

2. Success on the healing ladder requires total honesty with oneself. I often did not like what I was learning about myself; but trust me…honestly identify the causes of the problem you are examining. Identify your personal responsibility or all that is yours to claim honestly! Remember, you pay the consequences for the choices you make in the healing process.

3. Have you identified a problem area with you? Remember, you are the only one you can change or control how you allow others to affect you. You cannot control them…only you. Define specific changes you want to make and rank them as to priority; then write concrete goals for you. Don't forget to celebrate this discovery!

4. Are you a helper? Each time you have a contact with the person you are helping, check for something you may have done that you can possibly label as enabling or judging if you agree it is important. You may have identified something else to note here:

5. Do you feel uncomfortable or angry after you have 'helped'? Are you claiming only what is yours to claim? Remember, your responsibilities, your choices, your consequences to pay.

6. Should the helper 'encourage' a victim as to his/her relationship or responsibility to the perpetrator? Defend you answer.

VICTIM/ENABLER/HELPER? ADDENDUM

Is there not always a connection between a healing and a negativity? I have never heard of a positive experience that required healing. I believe it is imperative, therefore, to define and address the negative preventing healing in one's current life. Abuse is an uncomfortable wound. It is a topic not comfortable for the abused nor the helper to address openly with another human. I also recognize one may choose not to do the work required to heal. One of the two most important people in my life, chose the latter stating: "I don't like to think about bad things, I put that in God's hands"... and, in later years, tried to commit suicide multiple times.

I have been asked how to find a counselor and have answered with a suggestion stating that a good time to find someone for help is to search and identify that person when one does not feel the need for a counselor. However, I do not believe that option is always available.

VICTIM/ HELPER-- I do not support encouraging a victim to not deal with current negativity involving abuse; but rather to identify and heal or negate negative results he/she is experiencing today. As an example: I am pushed down a flight of stairs and have a broken leg as a result. I go to a doctor who tells me to heal the resulting pain by suggesting to 'forget it' or to 'bury the memory in which it was broken' and leaves the room telling me to make another appointment. I would turn and go to the doctor in the next office for my next appointment. I would also tell anyone else to do the same. Is telling someone to not address continuing pain the same as telling another not to heal? I also believe that, if at any time, I am required to re-experience an abusive scenario, I am, again in an abusive situation. Let's say, the doctor in the next office only asks me questions about the abusive scenario, questions such as: who pushed you ... where were you when you were pushed ... why were you there ... who was with you ... who did you tell ... forcing me to re-experience the emotional results, in addition to the physical, of the abusive incident and then walked out telling me to make the next appointment. I would go to the next office (assuming I could walk) instead. I would tell anyone else to do the same. How is one asking a victim of an abusive situation to re-experience it by asking questions regarding what cannot be changed by him/her not being abusive to the victim? The situation has already happened. The past cannot be changed in the present. Consequently, I identify the first doctor of defining me as a non-entity. And I describe the second doctor as abusing me by controlling me to re- experience the effects of the abuse by using the questions as the weapon. Perhaps it is always important to realize that without holding the proper credentials we, as helpers, may not be qualified to help with the physical results of abuse. Because neither of us can change the past and I personally do not hold the credentials to change the present physical results of the past nor do I desire to force another to stay in current negativity, I prefer to stay in the present tense when questioning a victim sitting in front of me.

Sometimes questions can be weapons; other times, the question asked can provide an 'ah hah moment' by suggesting taking a path not yet identified. The abusive experience may be holding insights to lingering unanswered questions. If another, when you are talking, has frequently described situations with the phrase: "it just doesn't make sense!"; you may be able to provide some answers by listening carefully over time as a friend of mine did for me. One day, after I said, " I just don't get it, it doesn't make sense", she asked if she could get personal and I gave my permission. She said: " I think this may be a possibility..." It was like I had been struck by lightning! I cannot say how long I sat there while scenario after scenario were going across my brain like cars on a train going by and each one, connected to the last and made sense! I do not believe I ever would have gone down the required path to obtain the answers those puzzle pieces showed me as the emotions the pieces triggered had been all-consuming. However, this conversation took place fifteen years after I started my healing process on the ladder, and I still had some contact with others within the past scenarios. I believe God oversaw the timing. I readily accept the possibility that, initially, the information would have sent me back to the pit if I would have had it on the ladder climb. Sometimes another who is not suffering the negativity of the unknown to the victim can more easily identify the forming picture and possibly definitions of existing secrets kept from the victim. However, timing can be extremely important in the healing process, which is why I choose to give the victim control of conversations.

The gift to me was that the 'possibilities' the puzzle pieces suggested by my friend offered me the ability to step into lives of significant others, as them in the scenario on the puzzle piece. (a tool I used frequently on the ladder climb when studying these same puzzle pieces but not able to fit them into the big picture). But, this time, my friend had apparently identified historic secrets I had not been told in their lives that caused negativity in my life. It helped me to re-examine the same puzzle pieces differently allowing my current struggles to become clearer...not better nor acceptable but making sense. It also helped in connecting with other pieces I had experienced but caused additional confusion as to how they fit into the big picture. Each of these frustrating pieces were quickly fitting into another easily and making the big picture identifiable. And, at the same time, verifying my friend's conclusions from my memory snippets I had shared. Suddenly the puzzle pieces were now easily filling in many blank spaces in my life-story puzzle causing the big picture to become clear and start to make total sense as I began to understand not only why each significant other in the various scenarios reacted differently than I but also provided insight as to their identifications of me! The latter allows me to honestly say today: If I were that person, I would feel the exact same way about me then and now.

Disappearing rapidly were the negative emotions I had experienced in continually struggling to identify my sins requiring forgiveness in addition to the confusion involved in labeling responsibilities I may have been required to claim. I was finally able to shelf the book containing the past pages because, although the results were not warm fuzzies, 2+2=4 because it all made sense to me. I put the closed book on the shelf, and turned into the present day taking a very deep breath with a goal to define how to polish any positive it holds... A gift a helper gave me who listened, cared for years, and then asked permission to provide me with knowledge to help me walk into a current day with positive goals, rather than force me to stay in the negativity of re-experiencing the pain in the abusive situation by trying to correctly answer questions in descriptions of a situation that is impossible to change because it is in the past. The insights resulted in allowing me to 'fight the case' of significant others who I had described as continually hurting me over the years because I now 'got it'; I now understand resulting behaviors and it no longer hurts me. And I also understand they made different choices over the years than I; we are at different places in the healing process and have different life stories; then and now.

A helper may have the opportunity to define insights required to experience the positive available in this day into and including the future. I needed to get concrete information I could use to help me make 2+2=4. I also had to gain the information to verify that I was now the person who could currently live in my environment believing I deserved the same respect given to others. I had to be worth the effort required, as I am the only human who can fight my battles in life. Sometimes, the answers do not provide warm, fuzzy, safe environments with others. Some stories require a special type of strength to live in certain environments with others because the results of some insights may not bring new scenarios with changed relationships for the better. Not everyone makes the same choices in handling their life stories. I believe, I did not have the strength required to get some answers earlier than I did. Understanding a situation does not always include making the situation more positive in which to exist. What the insights provided me years later was the ability to not allow current scenarios with the significant others of the past to create lasting negativity in this day. But, rather to recognize we have made different choices in our lives. Consequently, I am now able to close the book, put it on the shelf and turn into this day experiencing an understanding of the past negative and examining how my experience can possibly help others today.

I remember the shocking peace I felt the first time I experienced that result. I am so thankful the God I worship, and is my constant Ally, ' gets it'. By putting myself in the past negative scenarios in the others' positions, in addition to gaining an insight as to how their experience in the puzzle piece differed from mine, I can state that I 'get it' resulting in the pain and issues I held regarding the scenario to disappear. In like conversations today with significant others, rather than seeing God's armor as in a war; I picture myself with a raincoat on covering all but my face, hands, and feet allowing the negativities to simply fall over the raincoat and flow down the Solid Rock as I am on the Foundation. I readily understand I would probably be stating all in the same manner if I were the other making the choices apparently made in that current life. We all have, and still may be, living consequences for the choices made over the years. HELPER, I THINK THE BEST PATH TO FOLLOW WITH ANOTHER SHARING AN ABUSIVE SCENARIO IS TO ALLOW THEM TO BE THE ONE TO DIRECT THE CONVERSATION BACK TO THE ABUSIVE SCENARIO, WHEN I AM THE 'HELPER', I STRIVE TO KEEP MY QUESTIONS IN PRESENT TENSE i.e.: 'HAVE YOU IDENTIFIED A NEGATIVITY FROM THIS EXPERIENCE THAT IS PREVENTING YOU FROM IDENTIFYING TODAY AS POSITIVE? My part of the conversation then is in present and future tense. In discussing how the negative is impacting today, it may easily be the case that the individual decides to go back to the scenario and identify claiming and responsibilities, with any negativity current. Then check to see if guilt, forgiveness, etc. needs to be redefined. Perhaps, some or all an assignment for the inner room. Then, as is always the case with new insights, check for and define necessary steps he/she feels required to take with the defined negativities described in making a goal to achieve positive.

A helper might be the concrete other who is demonstrating caring by respectful listening without judging, perhaps not available any place else within the victim's daily environment. One who is choosing to begin the fight to heal needs strength to fight; and, probably, other steps are a necessity to gain the required strength. When I defined myself as not worth spitting on, I could only fight for others because they were worth the fight. I believe each victim deserves the time to change self-identity to agree with God's definition. God allowed that in the Bible; Job is an exceptionally long book; and I understand it to say God waited patiently. It was Job's 'friends' who made the battle more difficult by dictating and judging, in my opinion.

The healing process can never be identified as 'one size fits all'. A friend who is a policeman once told me that generally people at the same scene will each describe it differently because it affects people differently. I think the same could be said in any one of our life-story puzzle pieces. Consequently, the manner with which a current identified problem is addressed can be extremely important as it has the potential to increase a current negative rather than provide a positive. I have read explanations of possible negatives from a memory coming to mind; including re-experiencing physical feelings experienced in the past scenario. Not only that; but my life-story pages, past and present, have me convinced that the same statement may provide a positive for me today and a negative experience tomorrow depending on my present self-identified status; perhaps changed because I have experienced a negative trigger. I think it is always a good idea for a helper to wait to help until after listening to how the other defines his/her present status when in the conversation.

Have you ever described a Bible passage as speaking to you differently reading it at different times? I defined that experience as one of the neatest things about the Bible just the other day. Personal experience has taught me that the same Biblical passage can affect me totally differently dependent on the current situation and how I am self-describing as a result. The following is my experience as the victim: Consequently, as a helper in a conversation with a fellow believer who is an abuse victim/survivor, I am cautious and try to understand their current self-definition. Let me try to explain how a memory, or trigger, or the self-identification with which a person is standing right now in this conversation can be important: For instance**: 'God is always with you'**...If I am re-experiencing as a victim, being shamed and hating self, it is not helping me...God is 'watching this happening to me; has to be punishing me for?' ... increases my unrequired shame and guilt big time (the guilt and shame need to be defined and negated before reminding me that God is always with me and knows what is happening and all I have done. The steps I, personally use have been described within these chapters) ----or---- **'God is always with you'**...If I am experiencing being a survivor right now-- as good as others in my environment-- deserving of healing...helping...Ok, yes...you're right; I'm not going to let this trigger put me back on the ladder... let's do this; I am ready and am standing beside the most powerful Ally there is:----Satan, here I come, watch out!!!

It may identify how the helper can be of help instead of hinderance if the current position of the other can be identified by what he/she is stating. I believe the helper <u>never</u> knows the whole story of the other; it is possible neither person does. God is the One who does, which is why it may be wise for both to turn to Him early on and continuously throughout the climb. When a victim, I was unable to accept equality as a definition of me. Knowing that God was always with me was one reason I felt so much shame: at times hating self! However, when I started to feel equal, leaning into my anger as one capable of feeling equal and anxious to live the life I desired, I was able to be thankful there are no secrets from God. It was then that I wanted to learn and accept what He says regarding revenge and how He handles it. It was a true gift at that point in my healing process. Early in my healing process, you probably could have repeated to me a dozen times in one conversation that God loves me and that we all are equal at the foot of the cross and I would not have recognized the personal positive that it brings me today, defining self as a survivor rather than a victim.

It possibly can take quite a while before a victim can even believe he/she is worth the effort to even question the possibility of being loveable or worthy of anyone's time. Especially when there are rules being given by significant others. We do not have an x-ray clearly describing the emotive wounds resulting from an abusive experience. When I was climbing the healing ladder, an obvious choice was always to only step on one rung at a time; taking two or skipping one could result in devastating results. My suggestion, in working through this book is to start on page one and climb, one step at a time, looking up towards the Light rather than back down to the pit.

As believers, we each have One with us right now...every minute of every day Who knows every answer. He also knows what is necessary for us to know and do; but we must be open to His guidance. God gives us free will to make our choices with the rule that we pay the consequences. I am thankful that He gave me the strength to make choices for my walk in this life. And I am thankful that I finally chose to strive to follow God's lead with His definition as an equal to others within my environment. But I also am thankful that He patiently waited for me to turn to Him. He knew me; knew my self-identification and when to allow me to have insights; generally, a little at a time, allowing me to become the person I perhaps always was but had not identified. I question if He allows triggers of past scenarios to suddenly come because they contain unidentified tools that He needs me to use on the path chosen for me to walk. An unexpected revelation has been extremely helpful when Satan suddenly has appeared causing me to lean into the personal assurance of strength that God provides. The scenarios never change, just the way I identified them as my ability to look beyond me and view significant others grew with each insight. I began to stop turning to significant others for information I could not gain. And, by turning to God, also began using inner and outer strength I did not realize I had at my disposal to use for me as well as to help others.

Because God is always with His believers, I believe He knows me better than you and I combined. He knows the answer to each question I have had regarding my life, and I now recognize He knows which answers would be detrimental for me in my current daily walk. I also have concluded that when I was consciously deciding not to turn to His Word and find His desires for me, as His child, the devil was a happy camper. I, on the other hand, was totally frustrated in my search for answers and fighting for some self-worth.

Not only should it never be assumed that 'one size fits all'; but, neither can it be assumed that the healing process will be identical for each issue in one's life. One person's shared story may be one of many lasting over years of abuse, while another person experienced one scenario of abuse in his/her life. However, the results may be just as debilitating today for both.

I was constantly changing goals and thankful that I had, as it indicated growth. I, personally, pray I never stop growing as a child of God. It is a good idea to attempt to follow God's lead when in a helping role. When I finally chose to turn to Him for help, I realized I was starting to define my negativity and healing differently. Not only did experiences such as reactions to triggers allow me to recognize positives in insights rather than experiencing more bitterness; but I was also becoming much more independent and self-assured. The new sense of safety allowed me to readily look beyond; me, allowing me to study each scenario from the viewpoint of significant others within the puzzle piece that differed from my reactions. Studying His Word, I began to accept that He was and is not only with me as an Ally; but loves me and identifies me as an equal to others; and He also has plans for me. However, I could not accept a belief of His love and caring for me until I began to recognize I, myself, was beginning to identify worth in me as a fellow human to others; even when significant others disagreed. I began to not only recognize an inner strength; but was also surprised at feeling excited about the way I recognized He was providing me with answers; as well as gaining an understanding as to the possibility that it was best to not have answers to all questions. I then easily recognized that I was no longer a victim, but a survivor capable of protecting self from being victimized by others.

Do I believe I had the right to zero in on 'just me' when slipping and sliding in the pit and on the first ladder rungs? ..... Absolutely, I believe it is a necessity to define one's handicaps and assets properly as I was and still am the only human who experienced each piece of my puzzle. However, I also believe it was necessary to adopt God's definitions in applying what He was showing me, as a believer, to form and adapt. Until I was able to look beyond myself, and then turn to Him, willing to follow His guidance, I was unable to live the life I desired.

When in the pit, I easily defined myself as a panic-stricken child not capable of standing. However, had you worked with the adult me weekly as a fellow-employee at that time, you may not have recognized the 'other'. As adults, we can do an excellent job of living a facade. Consequently, I believe strongly that I can never trust that I maintain the ability to correctly define where another is in his/her healing process. My desire is that I will always assume they have not told me the most difficult pages in the story they are sharing. My goal in the helping role is to remember I do not know what the other has not shared. Therefore, I strive to respectfully honor his/her right to make the choices for which he/she is responsible to pay the consequences. I also hope I respectfully try to listen to his/her personal insights and perspectives.

I believe any time I am 'helping' another believer, we are both involved in spiritual warfare. Therefore, I hope I think before I talk... and continually see the person in front of me as God does---my equal. PLEASE consider this: If the devil is involved with spiritual warfare, he is an enemy of not only God; but you and me as believers who desire to follow God's path. God is the One always fighting the devil and God is the one who will always win the battle for us. When in a helper situation, I want to be a helper to the individual in front of me rather than being a help to Satan!

SURVIVOR-- I believe any survivor, would agree that, when sharing any part of our past-story pages, we do not want pity from others. We are strong and know how to stand up to Satan. We are thankful that we are living a different life than when we were climbing the ladder, a victim.

When climbing the ladder, an unwritten goal on each rung was the ability to hang on allowing me to stand on the next rung. If I was on the ladder, the past pages were in front of me. It was a requirement to gain insight as to what was going on with me. Early on the ladder, and unable to look beyond me; when examining the puzzle pieces, I was that victim reacting to the piece I was studying. Slowly, I gained the ability to look beyond me and realized not everyone in the piece had the same responses to the scenario, neither were they currently making the same choices as I. Consequently, I was not reacting to the negativity in the same manner. Turning to God for guidance, I could sense positive (insights I referenced as information to help me and others rather than experiencing the emotive bitterness). I also could often, and still do today: 'polish the positive'.

Off the ladder and standing in the Light, with use of the armor provided by God; knowing He was standing right beside me, I closed the past-life story and put the book on the shelf. I could breathe easier and be in the current day which provided the concrete. I no longer felt the need for others to help provide the concrete. I had the new self-identity that God helped me to claim on the ladder. I was able to use the inner strength to make decisions daily without the need for humans to provide verifications, as I was leaning into my new self-identity with God as my Ally.

However, I am not saying that, as a survivor one does not have battles. It is always extremely important within the healing process to remember that others make their choices and I make mine. Not everyone in a scenario makes the same choices nor does everyone react to the same situation in the same manner. I can only control me; and am not required to allow others to control me. When I am standing on the Foundation rather than ladder rungs, God is concrete when I use prayer for insight. It began to become clear to me, on the upper rungs of the ladder, that God was a better choice than humans for answers. God has helped me to realize that He knows and understands me better than any human, including me. Experience has taught me that He recognizes my personal need for 'concrete'. It no longer surprises me when a fellow human will show up and, in some way, verify what have just defined as an answer. Because I believe God knows all, and humans never do, I feel much more comfortable that I am striving to follow His direction when I begin with prayer. I am one who tends to want to fix it, fix it right now, and get on with life. However, you may also experience not getting answers to some questions, as is my experience. But I now am beginning to think perhaps it is better to not have some of the answers; just as my one friend and I decided that it was better for us to not have the answers when we were questioning at the time of her husband's funeral, many years prior. So, perhaps it is a not an issue to be identified to solve. I think that it is important to always remember that God is the only all-knowing one. It is easier to accept, however, as a survivor than it was when I was a victim!

ENABLER—It is my opinion that one may be enabling without realizing it. If you care for another, you want to help. Are you turning to the One for guidance? Then, are you constantly following His leading in conversations with the other? There have been times when I have labeled what I was doing for another as helping; however, years later, I question if I was enabling. It may be important to consistently monitor self in any given relationship. If you love another and feel you can help; it can be exceedingly difficult to look beyond and question if your 'help' is possibly supporting the other's choice to remain a victim rather than do the work to become a survivor.

GUILT

Wow...what a topic to choose to discuss! The idea causes me to consider visiting a doctor...perhaps one specializing in brain surgery would be an appropriate choice. However, in all honesty, I would be forced to admit the action would only be choosing to take another path of procrastination. So, let us begin our examination of guilt and the possibilities it may reveal.

I think responsibility, forgiveness and guilt are generally connected as most times all three of these issues fit in the same puzzle piece I am examining. Experience has taught me that, not only is guilt one of the most common factors in my personal healing process; but, to deal with my guilt, requires me to also deal with my responsibility before I step back off the ladder onto solid ground. To successfully be the person I wish to be, I must correctly identify and claim the responsibility assigned to me in situations I find myself day to day.

My experiences have often taught me that when I, too quickly, act based on my feelings of guilt; I am apt to be extremely inappropriate in my responses. Most of us probably have examined issues involving guilt in our lives. I do not know about you; but whenever I refer to myself in any way as a perfect person, others laugh. Consequently, working under the assumption that not one among us is perfect, let us assume that dealing with guilt is something we all have in common as we all have hurt and been hurt in some way dealing with others in our daily lives. When in such a situation, one may ascertain that the situation needs to be examined to see if an apology is required. However, is the responsibility to be assigned to me? For me, always an important question to consider in puzzle examinations and observations.

My healing process has become likened to a second nature of sorts and I am consistently using it as a tool. It has taught me that guilt has oftentimes been an unrecognized detriment to me. Therefore, anytime I am required to examine a past or current situation I am in, it would behoove me to search for a sense of guilt. It seems for me, personally, it is generally a key piece in any puzzle I examine in my life. In any case, whatever the trait, perhaps certain questions might always be appropriate for anyone.

Is it possible that acting too quickly when one is hurting may escalate a given situation? If so, before acting, it may be beneficial for all if one identifies the role guilt plays in the situation. Is it then necessary to examine one's role in the picture honestly and carefully to determine if the guilt is a result of a responsibility which he/she is required to claim? However, if in fact, it is determined honestly that the guilt one has accepted is unreasonable, would it not be inappropriate for one to act from the source of guilt? Would such a situation present an ideal time to turn, walk away, and peel a layer or, at minimum, carefully examine the situation before acting or reacting?

Is it not possible, if one readily accepts misguided guilt, he/she would likely have difficulty protecting self? Is it not possible misguided guilt could also be used as a toxic self-inflicted weapon? When recurring concepts and/or individuals are recognized as common pieces of the puzzles in one's life; it is wise to do some introspection. I do not know about you, but I know I manage to get myself into plenty of situations within a given day in which I am required to claim guilt without adding misguided guilt into the mix!

Or could it also be possible that, if I choose not to claim my feelings of guilt responsibly, I may put forth the effort to transfer the guilt unreasonably to another? If I recognize the hurt of another is in any way a result of a behavior of mine, it makes sense to me that I am then required to respond differently than if I cannot label any responsibility for the feelings or behavior of another. As easy as this sounds and as much sense as it makes to me; the truth of the matter is that it is difficult to do when in the middle of a hurtful situation. For me, emotions such as anger often get in the way. In any case, might it be more important than readily recognized, that taking time to properly label one's responsibility of claiming guilt in a situation with others may be of value when examining issues involved in the daily relationships in our lives?

I believe it is entirely possible those of us who have abuse in our life's story have a more difficult time defining guilt appropriately than others. I believe that, within the definition of abuse, a 'teaching of guilt' is <u>always</u> present. Because many of us have been taught, at some point, that we are bad in some way; not as good as our abuser or, perhaps anyone else on the face of this universe, the consequence of such a scenario is obvious: we are responsible, therefore required to accept guilt.

Another factor that may influence the examination of guilt might be an inner desire to follow church doctrine. Could it be that certain definitions of church teachings may present added challenges in the ability to claim responsibilities? My personal experience causes me to answer this question affirmatively pertaining to guilt. Examining my personal experience in the church environment, I recall times being in gatherings and feeling as though I was being beaten or, at minimum, frightened and needing to confess something. Oftentimes, I was not certain as to what the something was; however, did not question its existence as I felt required to feel guilty.

As an adult I began peeling the layers of my life. I found each layer represented another reflection demanding an honest inspection of my role in accepting responsibility; thereby, enabling me to climb higher into the Light. I oftentimes realized I had been overwhelmed with misguided guilt and in a position to question how I could ever become the person I desired. However, it is amazing how the tools I use in my healing process are adaptable and pertinent to any situation in which I find myself.

Today I still find, when I am triggered, to go back to the healing ladder if guilt is identified; I may use the sense of guilt as a starting point in my examination. In doing so, the whole process is apt to be very short-lived, and seldom will I feel the need to ask for help finding my way back. If I label that I am claiming misguided guilt, the puzzle pieces are identified much more quickly as being a common thread within the layers of my story. Consequently, labeling and controlling the guilt issue quickly in situations, allows me the benefit of less struggles and less required time examining within the healing process; thus, negating the negative and propelling the positive!

I am discovering that by reaching this point, I am consistently much more focused on the positive and walking in the Light rather than struggling and feeling surrounded by negativity. An appropriate question at this point may be: How effective can I possibly be in following God, or accomplishing my personal goals, if I am remaining in a place constantly surrounded by negativity? A constant goal is that I use the strength in me to accept the responsibility to examine myself honestly within any situation in front of me and to accomplish that which requires action within me.

Perhaps an honest examination of guilt and the resulting responsibility it evidences, could be an important step in achieving a desired relationship with God. It appears whether I label myself as victim or as perpetrator in a situation, every time I turn away and take quiet time for honestly examining myself while praying for guidance, I am taught something new about me. Although it is not unusual to identify changes required within me, the more often I take time to consciously work to claim responsibility to make the identified changes a reality, the more the scales indicate additions to the positive side. Making necessary changes within myself often results in less negativity within my thoughts, presenting me with a time for not only giving thanks to God, but a cause for celebration for me.

SUPPLEMENT to GUILT

1. Have you been able to identify an issue or concept you discovered as often being a piece that fits into many of the various puzzles your life story provides? I have found, once I zero in on changes I need to make around these, like guilt and responsibility for me, my days are much better; I feel good about my day. Have you discovered topics or issues falling into this category?

2. You may be able to make groupings in your list. Then, perhaps you will be fortunate enough to be able to make a goal to change more than one issue on your list at the same time! When I can do this, I do not have to spend as much time on the healing ladder! Is this possible with your list?

3. Does anything on the list represent misguided responsibility you have claimed? Did you take the blame for something that was not your fault? If so, is that ok with you? Did you take the blame for all that was your fault? If so, list any changes you want to make in you.

4. Remember, it won't help you in the present to find things you need to change, if you choose to not work to change. If something is not ok with you the way it is, and now is a good time to write a concrete goal, would an explanation of what it will look like, and three things you are going to do to make that change a done deal be a good place to start?

5. What are you going to do to celebrate today?

Guilt Addendum

I chose to look at the word 'guilt' in dictionaries for students. After reading the definitions three or four times, I decided it is no wonder I struggled with guilt for years. It is a particularly difficult struggle when the 'something' <u>does</u> outrage the moral <u>and</u>/or physical senses of the individual struggling to define the required definition of his/her guilt for the breach of conduct he/she 'committed'. But that is never the <u>only</u> issue present in an abusive scenario. The guilt is likely interlocked with other emotions and/or issues (possibly unidentifiable). It is important to recognize that a victim of abuse has likely been shamed and taught he/she is at fault. An issue one may be defining quite differently as a survivor or an adult dealing with childhood abuse, in which anger can then easily be added to the entwined emotions being experienced.

One choice I made immediately upon high-school graduation was to avoid 'religious everything' I could...studying, church gatherings, etc. I defined my life as one I did not want to continue. And, although I was a believer, chose to turn my back on all that (including God) because of my guilt in not possessing the skills required to be a "good Christian". My self-concept contained only negatives. I knew I was a sinner and required to forgive others; but also, and equally important, I was required to define all my sins and ask God for forgiveness for each one. I understood it as rules that defined my eternity. And I defined my life as one full of sins. However, probably because I was such a terrible and sinful person, I could not describe most of <u>my</u> sins. So, I decided to take my future into my own hands and control me to at least provide the life I pictured as successful. Consequently, I spent the next thirty years of my life living the consequences of my choices. In those years of my life, I felt that my choices allowed me to have a life unlike the one I had prior. I recognized I could use personal skills to be respected by others in the daily work-fields I chose. I was able to save money and pay for college. I was able to use my identified strength to fight for others. Not me, personally as much, however, because I now realize I had buried all those emotions and memories and was making choices to live in an unidentified-as-abusive relationship for twenty- five years; but my life 'outwardly' fit my definition of the life I wanted. Even though I was consciously aware of unidentified issues preventing me from being able to accept the self-identity that would correspond to the 'outward life' I was living.

It was in my healing-ladder experience that I defined and labeled the results of choices I had made. Climbing each rung, I consciously felt I was looking up rather than back toward the slime in the pit; consequently, I became aware of the Light reaching down the ladder rungs. I also began realizing God was my definition of the Light I could see coming from the Foundation at the top of the ladder reaching down the rungs to me. I began turning to God, rather than humans, for insights in examining the pieces of the puzzle. God gifted me the ability to 'see beyond me' in my examinations allowing me to define myself as well as my responsibilities differently. Then, I was able to see more of the total picture in addition to my perspective of the scenario on the piece being examined. I began using Him as my Ally in gaining identifications and insights while trying to remember that He sees me as a loved child of His and equal to all others.

Today, I can easily identify pieces, throughout all those years, which show God waiting patiently for me to turn to Him; and only giving me helpful information to the point that it would not prevent me from claiming responsibilities in my daily life which were required of me. Thus, today I can honestly say that I am thankful for my life story. I do not believe God forced choices upon me; but rather He gifts me control to make choices for which I then pay the consequences. For way too many years, I made choices turning to every place <u>except</u> Him for guidance and insight; consequently, I paid the consequences of <u>my</u> choices. My life experience has told me that I do not stand alone in any current negativity I have experienced from past scenarios.

If you are a helper who has not experienced a life which has taught you that you are unworthy, worse than everyone else in your environment, and whatever happened you deserved; please be very respectful to the ones who have experienced it. Please respect their opinions without arguing; their opinions will probably shift some as identifications and clarifications of present-day resulting negativities are identified. But they may have realized that a current trigger has tossed them back down to a self-identification of a victim instead of a survivor; consequently, they are now in a negative place rather than the positive they have been experiencing. An unidentified negative affecting my life today is not going to be voided if I am unaware of it. Unpleasant as it may be to re-experience, it could be required for me to accomplish God's will for me in the present. I would like to give you an example by explaining what a helper of mine did when I was the one screaming in his office in this situation:

I was in my Pastor's office screaming at him that I could not feel God's presence, because HE probably was not there! The Pastor interrupted me and said: 'excuse me, help me out here; I'm confused... are you saying that you are yelling at a Being you don't believe exists?' ... This is the helper I want to be when helping someone who is where I was. Let me explain why: 1. Pastor respected me: "Excuse me" (it stopped me). 2. "Help me": (traded positions by assigning me to help him and he is allowing me the gift to identify self by explaining me to him. 3. "I'm confused" (I am confused also...but am no longer 'the victim' because his request has given me a much different role...helper (respected by prior 'excuse me') and controller (now I'm helping another understand so I must identify it to explain it to another; a process in which I have the opportunity to examine and identify and have the gift of an equal to support me in gaining insight to possibly prevent future negativities or turning this one into a positive by giving us both valuable information).

It can be assumed that this conversation is between two Believers: Let's have the current victim be the same person in the same situation but with a different helper: Helper interrupts: 1. "

What? I know you, and I know you don't believe that!" (yes, I do! ... that is why I am here, and I Do/Did believe that...I am not going to help you beat me up nor negate my experience. So, I now have two choices...both degrading to me.) 2. "Why?" (I am continuing to be a victim and I did not want to be in the negative situation I am still in and in the same place as when I walked in the door, only now I am also defending why I believe God is not there.) 3. " Well, you know that's not true."

I believe that both helper and other dealing with abusive scenarios are on the battlefield of spiritual warfare and that Satan is dipping the spears into self-identity, guilt, forgiveness, sin, anger, blah blah... all often unidentified fears and threats to prevent survivors from leaning into their strength to stay on the path following God's leading. I identify myself as a survivor and I know that, when I sense that self-identification is being threatened, I tend to lean into anger to fight. The victim generally does not experience anger because he/she/ accepts lacking self-worth as a truth when currently experiencing a situation which is verifying that self-definition.

The helper may be tempted to start with a statement I might want to say: "Oh, so, what we're going to do in this conversation is fight on the side of Satan?"....(true??...of course...BUT, how is that helping this fellow survivor, now 'victim' identify this trigger for what it is and walk out of the door after having used the sword of the armor of God against the devil?) A victim is <u>not</u> capable of doing that generally! I believe, if the current identification of the one asking for help is recognized correctly and respect is provided with each question and comment, the survivor may walk out the door rather than the victim who walked in. The survivor has already won many battles by obtaining the self-identification. But when judging that 'victim' he/she is joining other abusers by criticizing self. That is probably why he/she has experienced the trigger by Satan's dart. I, as a helper certainly would prefer to stand next to God in this conversation than to stand next to the devil! I do not ever want to help Satan by encouraging a fellow survivor coming to me for help to attack or judge that 'victim' within her/him. Neither would I ever hope to, in any way, encourage the survivor to negate that life's page...how is that not negating the other suggesting an identity of non-entity? Obviously, the trigger contains <u>something</u> important enough to affect his/her present day! My history defines who and what I am today. I have made my choices and I have experienced the consequences. How would you identify one saying you need to negate a life page at any time? When that is the action taken, any good is buried with the bad. I am not the only one who has experienced that result.

When I am experiencing a negative trigger and asking for help; I am experiencing it as the victim possibly both physically and emotionally. A situation which can easily require spending time back on the healing-ladder again with added guilt, blah blah ... or not. I believe that Pastor allowed me to continue to stay in that scenario to identify the negative and change it into positive as a survivor. Please allow me to continue to make the choices in my life for which I will be paying the consequences. I prefer to be proud of who I am today as the survivor, rather than being ashamed of my victim identification, in asking for help, I believe it can be used to give me and others insight. Besides, blank pages in the book of one's life story are not positively inspiring. I trust I will never agree to void the victim me in any manner, as that would be verifying the worthlessness of that part of me also. Consequently, an assignment given me to 'bury' or not address that part of my life is an invitation for battle; but, also, will force me to stay in the victim scenario with the victim label. I prefer the victim me equal to the survivor me as in God's eyes...I will fight hard today to agree with that definition allowing the 'victim' me to be the teacher in this current day when I have been assigned the role of helper. My experiences on the Foundation with past triggers have taught me that they often come to me because there is something in that scenario I have yet to identify and use to help others.

Yes, that is all it took for me to 'snap back' to the present that day in the Pastor's office. However, this Pastor knew me quite well and recognized that I would probably react the way I did; it is a lot easier for me to give and receive help from others with whom I have an established relationship. But if that is not the case; I as a helper am always going to try to ask questions in a manner which defines us as equals. Also, in a way in which I am not defining issues, goals, or any requirements necessary for the other to accomplish because I always know for a fact that I will never have all the information he/she does regarding this conversation. The manner with which the Pastor asked me the question was an important example for me to use as a helper today. He did not 'talk down' to me and he allowed me to define the unidentified issue dictating the negativity I was experiencing. (Only two beings have knowledge of everything in my life story; and God knows more than I!) However, I may not use this exact approach with another with whom I have no relationship prior to this conversation. When I am a survivor, I surely am worth being treated as an equal because, if for no other reason, God defines me as such! So, anyone better watch out because I may be also angry about how I was treated when believing all the negativity abuse teaches and am still required to talk to you about it because I have been triggered and am experiencing negativity because of it! So, here is my conclusion drawn from this as a helper. I try hard to identify how I can help and still respect. An IMPORTANT thing to ALWAYS remember, however, is any question I ask another referencing a situation that they have described, is forcing him/her to stay within that situation to answer.

Here is what I intend to do the next time a fellow believer comes to me for help and is in a triggered situation. I believe, in this conversation, we would both agree with the following: 1. We are God's children. 2. He loves us and sees us as equal to all. 3. He has a path for us to follow. 4. He has gifted us with freedom of choice accompanied with resulting consequences of the choices made. 5. If we choose to follow His leading, we have the added gift of the armor of God to use against the enemy defined as Satan. SO: victim and/or survivor: I would lean into 1-4 with anything I say to him/her.

Because it is important to remember that we each will turn and step back into our individual present lives after we close this conversation. My desire, as a helper, is to not add to any threats. However, if I am comfortable and if I can identify the other as having the strength in this present conversation to use words like armor; warfare, Satan, darts, etc., I may take advantage of any anger verbalism they have used to assume I can go deeper and address spiritual warfare; possibly even addressing the anger issue with something like maybe: "I know, when I personally feel angry, at least I can recognize I have a sense of strength I don't have when I am a victim (an advantage I have with past 'victim-year' pages; but maybe you can tweak the idea to use). So, the question may become: How to use the anger...by zeroing in on the past that cannot be changed...or...using the strength to face the devil and yell (my choice, maybe not another's) and pray staying on the path following my chosen Ally. After all, IF # 5 is true; and we both believe there is a God, and a Satan, and a spiritual-warfare possibility, then why not assume that we have made the devil our enemy by turning to God. Consequently, Satan is going to dip the dart into the container holding the most vulnerable characteristics we have before firing it. My guess is that any believer with a history of abuse in a situation fitting this description is probably (as is generally the case with me) dealing with unrequired guilt and forgiveness and unidentifiable sin. Consequently, I would, as a helper (and me as the 'victim' if I am able), think of the following story I have made up for this purpose: If I touch you and you fall down a flight of stairs; I am, immediately going to feel terrible, extremely guilty ... blah...blah... blah! And, I have no problem identifying my guilt and responsibility for the pain you are suffering. But here today in this conversation, we are struggling to identify a guilt issue? Shouldn't that indicate some type of a negativity within a person that is non- existent if it cannot be labeled??? If, we can agree on that, then now, perhaps the anger is all that is left in this conversation to address. A question I, as the helper, would prefer the survivor identify and answer, perhaps in the inner room, if not with me...would be: Am I going to use my anger by examining a trigger that cannot be changed <u>or</u> stay with God beside me as my Ally and face the devil as my enemy using God's Word and my prayer. Which choice offers the best consequence? (REMEMBER, THE ONE WHO DEFINES THE CHOICE PAYS THE CONSEQUENCES OF THE CHOICE.)

Today I, generally, can lean into my strength and not accept the self-definitions on the darts Satan sends flying my direction. I prefer to use the chats I have with God for that because HE is the only other with me in each puzzle piece of my life. And guess what, in working a puzzle, every piece is connected to another piece required to see the 'whole picture'. Therefore, others do not have access to my answers.

I am also very thankful for the 'concrete' caring and honest others God has provided for support and help in defining answers HE was, and still is, providing in my puzzle. God gave them, and still does today, the ability to listen with discernment when helping me to identify present lingering negativities that can be changed into positives in this day if I choose to do so. ..... People who say things like: "It sounds like possibly ...Could this be preventing you today from...How do you think you could use this knowledge to help another today?" But I am also able to use my inner strength and positive self-identity to turn <u>from</u> another for help if they define who I am, how I should feel or not feel, or my issues that 'need to be fixed and how'; because I prefer the self-identity of survivor to victim. I have also learned it is important to remember (in the guilt and forgiveness issues, especially) that I am the only person who is making the choices in my life and paying the consequences for each one at this moment, not the other humans in my life. They are making their choices and paying the consequences. I am the only one I can control and, hopefully, I am turning to God to do it. He 'gets me'...I am a child of His...He was always there waiting patiently for me to turn to Him. And trust me; turning to Him is a choice enabling any believer to be a survivor in a safer and more respectful and pleasant life in which one can choose to live with a self-description of a child of God who He defines as an equal to all others rather than existing in acceptance of one's self-identity from significant other humans who may disagree with God's description.

I found it a requirement to label my emotions and carefully define claiming responsibilities in each puzzle piece in my inner room. I discovered early that I was the only one who could do the examining because I was the only one who lived each piece of the big puzzle. No other human experienced every scenario or the emotions present. I now, looking back, I easily recognize the importance of examining and labeling responsibility for guilt honestly and correctly. It is not unusual in life to define new goals after examinations. (My current life-experience is that x-rays generally precede surgery.)

For me, personally, before I could live the life I desired daily; I first had to take the time to carefully examine pieces and honestly define and address guilt and forgiveness using any applicable additional clues that helped me gain true insight. I believe, in abuse scenarios, unrequired guilt is always an issue that possibly can be lurking around unidentified, especially if the victim is struggling to define self-sin. (If he/she is required to struggle to define sin he/she committed, can you agree it is likely the issue being identified here is unrequired guilt?) I knew I was the one doing the work and I would be the one to live the consequences of the choices I was making. If following God's will is my goal, my honesty to me and faith in His definitions and guidance are requirements to walk with strength provided by the armor He provides for the ability to stand regardless of the darts that are sure to come. When they do; I try to remember to identify them as verifications that I am following God on the right path. Otherwise, I do not believe the devil would be as attentive to choices I make. My current goal in my life pages is to verify God is the Ally I choose to stand beside daily.

FORGIVENESS

An appropriate preface for the discussion of forgiveness could easily be the same as guilt...wow...what a subject! I have questioned many possibilities pertaining to the topic because, upon realizing forgiveness presented a threat to me, I knew the search demanded my honest inspection. As I climbed the healing ladder, I began to realize that often situations I examined in which the concept of forgiveness was a piece of the puzzle, the juxtaposition of forgiveness and the emotions I experienced with the recognition of its presence in the scenario at hand, simply did not make sense to me.

Because I held the opinion for years struggling on the healing ladder that I was not yet strong enough to deal with the concept of forgiveness; I kept procrastinating, not wanting to begin the required examination. The bad news is that it probably extended my time on the healing ladder by years; the good news is that, when I finally 'took the plunge' and attacked it, I had experience in using the tools I have presented.

Is it not possible that the word triggers a memory of some sort for each of us? Are you in the same position I was, unconsciously believing forgiveness is not <u>only</u> always required; but always looks the same? Would you have as difficult a time as I defining the word to enable you to effectively use it in your healing process? The thought occurred to me that it was extremely important to do so. Realizing how often forgiveness was involved in my examining and working with the various puzzle pieces, I began to ask others to define the word, particularly if it came up in conversations. I was initially surprised that, rather than a definition, the responses involved stuttering and stammering (however, often followed by fascinating conversations and insights).

In day-to-day living, involvement with people requires me often to apologize for something such as walking out of another's office with his/her pen in my hand. I take it back, apologize; no big deal, forgotten. ... done deal. Perhaps you are helping me clear the table after dinner at my house. You drop a plate and break it; feeling terrible, you apologize, and I respond with, "It's ok, don't worry about it", forgotten. ... done deal.

However, if forgiveness is a rule of life an individual feels required to follow in all situations, the possibility exists that one's life experiences may be such that the act of forgiving another and/or accepting apologies from another takes on a whole different dimension in certain situations.

Have you ever felt required to give/accept forgiveness and then felt an inexplicable anger or fear knowing a piece of you had just been stolen? You felt controlled or beaten by something you could not identify? When I am in a situation I define as critical in my healing process, I have recognized a need to ask for definitions of important words to me (i.e., forgive), particularly if I sense a need to protect myself within the given situation. I am aware of a situation in which a neighbor man was inappropriate to a young child and the parent called the young child to the door while telling the child to accept the man's apology. Have you ever felt that to give or to accept another's apology, you must give up a part of yourself to another to control?

Let us assume that my definition of forgive, regarding a current issue in which we are involved, is totally different than yours. I have wronged you resulting in you feeling threatened in some way. I say, "I wish you would forgive me".... Have I claimed responsibility for anything? You immediately say, "I forgive you". Is forgiving an issue that protecting self may require one to act by taking a breath or 'sleeping on it' instead of automatically reacting?

Does the world in which we live demand that we accept the possibility that our associates and friends may have a life story <u>not</u> comparable to ours? How important is such a possibility? If the common rule to be accepted is forgiveness, is it possible one's life experience could profoundly affect one's reaction to the topic? For instance, what if the aggressor is: the drunk driver who killed his son/ the group leader who sexually abused him as a young boy/ the boss who required sexual favors of her, a single mom, as a requirement to keep her job?

Is it possible that, in situations in which forgiveness is involved, the assumption should always be made that the possibility exists the person to whom you are talking may be impacted by what you say in a manner you would not normally imagine? If so, does not such a possibility require each of us to spend time carefully considering our acceptances and beliefs regarding the concept of forgiveness as well as how we present them to another? I began looking at somewhat non-threatening scenarios in my struggle to identify how I felt about the concept of forgiveness...a task still on the table and in my puzzle pictures. Let us look at situations together.

My guess is that you have been in this situation often as have I:

1-- two young siblings or classmates are squabbling.

2-- I, the adult, go to the aggressor and tell him/her an apology is due the other.

3-- The aggressor states an apology.

4-- I tell the victim, in some manner, that it is a done deal.

When considering the many years that I have been involved in such a scenario, I was totally surprised at my recent findings...let us examine together:

#1--squabbling-- Could it be possible my assumptions could have been somehow skewed by the possibility of a prior situation between the two which was unknown to me? What lesson did I just teach to both?

#2--apologize-- Is it possible when two are squabbling, the aggressor in the current situation does <u>not</u> owe the other an apology? What lesson did I just teach to both?

#3-- apology given-- Why? ... because I demanded? ... because a penalty would be the consequence of no apology? ... because he/she felt badly and was claiming responsibility? What lesson did I just teach to both?

#4--done deal-- What does this mean? Was each taught the same lesson or different ones? What lesson did I just teach?

Is it possible, that our adult lives are, in many ways, repetitions of our childhood experiences? Is it possible in our daily lives as adults with seemingly no time for introspection, we may grow into a tall child rather than an adult, having made no changes in who and what we believe or accept as a human being living in an environment with others? In our adult relationships, are not the same childhood situations transpiring; particularly when the same significant others are involved? I do not know about you, but I was rather shocked to realize that the young-child scenario described is pertinent to current pages in my life story. It was extremely helpful when I started applying the outline the above scenario offers to my life situations today using the same tools that I have used throughout my healing process.

The first realization was that I was shocked to realize that the rules by which I acted, and some that I still feel obligated to follow involving forgiveness, are presented within the scenario. I began using my healing-process tools in the outline the scenario offers by placing myself in the various positions. I began to realize my personal reactions and choices were, oftentimes, extremely toxic for me. The insights have given me direction as to changes I have made in claiming responsibilities and in rejecting misguided guilt. Let us take some time to adjust the questions somewhat. Hopefully, you will be able to discover some useful tools to apply in examining and in putting your puzzle together that will speed the process considerably.

It might be helpful if you can apply the following considerations to a current or past situation in which issues with another adult and forgiveness may be pieces in the puzzle. Let us also assume that the 'hurt' is not 'hitting' because, after all, we <u>are</u> adults; so, does this mean that the 'hurt' goes much deeper than a punch, possibly affecting the forgiveness issue profoundly?

Let us make you the aggressor:

#1--two squabbling-- aggressor hurts victim...Good! You have been working on your healing process and you <u>finally</u> have been able to use your strength to stand up for yourself! But are you silently punishing yourself for being bad? Is a voice in your head judging your behavior; is the voice that of a significant other, or is it your voice?

#2--you must apologize-- If you owe me an apology, does not that suggest you are to accept guilt? Have you ever apologized; but did so not knowing why; or, perhaps with a sense of an inexplicable personal loss...you just felt it was a requirement? If this assumption would accurately describe you in the situation, is it then possible that you have claimed guilt? Is it also possible that the guilt could be misguided... have you possibly claimed guilt that is the responsibility of another to claim? By claiming guilt, could you possibly be bringing toxicity into the present environment?

#3--you apologize-- How often in your life do you apologize? Is asking for forgiveness involved? For what are you guilty? Is it possible that you, the aggressor, and the victim may define either/or the guilt and the forgiveness differently; what about claiming and/or responsibility? How important would that be? Would it change the picture if your definitions are not the same?

#4--it is a done deal-- Do you believe that it is a done deal when you apologize...sometimes, always, never? How important is it that your definitions are agreed upon first? How important is it that the victim accepts the apology? Why? Are you prepared to not receive recognition for your apology? Are you prepared to not have your apology be accepted? How important is it to always remember that you are the only one you can change in any given situation?

Did you claim anything here that you can label as misguided? If so, please do not be too discouraged. Only yesterday I did just that; but all day today I have been on solid ground and in a positive place. Once you become comfortable doing this work, positive results appear very quickly.

Now let us make me the aggressor--you are the victim. Because I think it is not uncommon for one in such a scenario to be working on a healing process and the other choosing to not make such a choice, let us assume in the situation you are on the healing ladder and I am choosing not to change my ways. I commonly am the aggressor in our dealings...perhaps it has been a common scenario over the years for us to squabble and you to feel guilty.

#1-- I have hurt you. I must apologize. -- Perhaps I note you have backed away from me. I want it the way it was, so I apologize. Do you believe anyone has ever apologized to you without believing they were wrong? Have you ever felt an apology was something else? Have you ever felt you have slidden down the healing ladder after hearing or reading an apology from a significant other and not understood why?

#2-- I apologize-- I may say something like: "I am sorry you think I was wrong." Who is doing what with responsibility/claim/guilt/control here? Did I claim any responsibility? Did I use my apology as a weapon? What are you going to do with my apology?

#3-- It is a done deal-- As far as I am concerned, it probably is a done deal...after all, I apologized, right? Are you and I using the same definition of forgive? So, how do you feel now? Do you feel guilty for something? Do you feel it is your responsibility to consider it a done deal because I apologized? If the situation were reversed and you were apologizing to me in this situation, would you have said the same things? Why? Did the apology add another layer of toxicity onto you in any way? Are you easily defining forgiveness? Did you claim in a healthy manner or did you accept something that is the responsibility of another like me, the aggressor, for instance?

Do you and I have responsibilities to claim? If so, are we both claiming responsibilities only ours, individually, to claim? Do you believe you are the only one you can change/control? Have you accepted, or claimed, anything in this scenario that is misguided? This may be an excellent time for you to check for any changes you label as required of you before you are able to achieve your end goal. You may also find you are required to write a couple concrete present goals for use in future episodes between you and me.

It was in examining the forgiveness topic when I discovered how important it was for me, personally, to examine pronouns used by people, including me. Do you think pronouns used by us may reveal our (conscious or perhaps unconscious) definitions of responsibility and claiming? If one is experiencing inexplicable guilt after another has offered an apology, might it be advantageous to examine pronouns used?

I do not know about you; but I realized that I usually expect an apology to begin with the words: "I am sorry that **I** ____." Let us examine deeper yet possible apologies I may offer to you assigning me as the aggressor, so I am filling in the blank in the apology: "I am sorry that _____".

"I called you too late to come to the movie."
Am I not claiming responsibility in this apology?

"When Pete asked me where you were, I had to tell him you called and said you would not come."
Am I still claiming responsibility? Has anything else shifted?

"You upset Pete because you didn't come."
Have I just added another missile to my arsenal?

Is it possible that pronouns used in an apology and the placement of each pronoun within the apology may be key to the individual's claiming of personal responsibility or claiming nothing; perhaps, even shifting responsibility to the other? What has changed between "I am sorry that I...", and "I am sorry that you..."? If I am accepting or claiming something as belonging to me, then I say it is I/me/my/mine/our/we/us...If, on the other hand, I am not claiming it; but, rather stating another did it, I say it is you/your/yours/their/they. Is it possible that the use of pronouns in any discussion could hold a higher level of importance than previously noted?

Is it possible that I do not stand alone in having ignored the impact of the concept of forgiveness, not only in my own life, but in others? Am I the only one who is required to question how I handle situations involving forgiveness with children as well as with other adults involved within the pages of my life story? Is it possible that I have a responsibility that I have not previously labeled involving significant others?

Since I, personally, have examined this, I think it is possible using pronouns as a tool in examining any situation has kept me in the light instead of being required to step back on the healing ladder.

Within the given scenario, are the responsibilities of each individual regarding claim/blame/apologies/forgiveness identical or different? Do all parties involved agree as to definitions? Do the answers to these questions play a part in your sense of well-being? How important is it to always keep in mind that the only person you can control is you? If the latter is true, would a change in your approaching any given situation with me, the aggressor, be a healthy concept to examine for you to be in the Light when dealing with me?

Is it possible that, when forgiveness is a piece of a puzzle one examines in the healing process, the same questions and tools may be applicable to the forgiveness piece as to the other pieces? Does the possibility exist that if forgiveness is a part of a puzzle, toxicity may also be present? If so, would identification of responsibility also be wise? Does responsibility change with the situation, or does the same individual have the same responsibility in varying situations?

Forgiveness was a topic I knew I had to recognize, study, and use; I labeled it as fundamental in my goal of existing in the Light. However, it was, for me, possibly the most threatening item required of me for the closure I was seeking. Consequently, I believe my personal struggle on the healing ladder took the length of time it did because I kept laying the forgiveness piece of any scenario, I was examining back on the table instead of discovering how it fit into the puzzle. Therefore, I also postponed defining changes I needed to make for my current page to be positive. For instance, I consciously avoided anything religious because I did not want someone else telling me how I was required to forgive and deal with the sin issue. I already was dealing with it... every day of my life...no one could make me feel any more a sinner; and I already was convinced that I was required to forgive...always... to be the person I wished to become. I knew all of that; but was not strong enough to deal with it yet. I believed the cost to me would be too high a price to pay. It took years of struggling to finally be able to believe my thinking may have been terribly skewed.

I know there are numerous times in any given life-story layer in which I was, and am currently, required to give apologies and to request forgiveness. I have a responsibility to recognize those times and claim my behavior and the apology required, not dependent upon an acceptance, because I am responsible to claim my own behavior and my personal choices.

I think the problem, in my case, may have been that my original belief was that forgiveness would be required for me to offer, or to accept, in <u>any</u> given situation as I so readily accepted guilt in any situation. Therefore, discovering these tools to use when examining situations involving forgiveness was life changing for me.

I believe forgiveness is required of me. In my view, forgiveness does not always mean it is a done deal, if done deal means forgotten or no more effects because of the situation. Some things are never forgotten and sometimes we experience triggers; however, if forgiveness is a topic, then the happenings are in the past and cannot be changed. We are never able to change what has already transpired, and sometimes we are not able to forget. I think that the past is, and always will be, whatever it was. However, we do have control over the present. Although I was, and still am, required to deal with the past; I believe I cannot accomplish my life's purpose if I am controlled by the past.

In my studying of God's Word in the past couple years I noted He said that vengeance is His. Somehow that is extremely helpful to me. It allows me to open the door and shove out toxicity. It helps to clear my mind, enabling me to think about current day-to-day activities as the past layers are closed and saved within my life-story book on the shelf. However, many puzzle pieces are contained within those pages; therefore, I am thankful I have the ability today to take the book down from the shelf to open or close it at will. Then, to put it back on the shelf, turn, and walk into today and sleep well tonight with no nightmares. I am glad my book is available to me at any time. After all, my life story defines who and what I am; to deny its contents would be to deny my essence. In my view, the concept of denying one's essence is surely <u>not</u> included within a correct definition of forgiveness!

There was a long period of time in which I allowed my personal fear of forgiveness to control the pages of my life story. I was scared; it was as though I likened forgiveness with being forced to give a part of who I was becoming to another to control. Although I currently am cautious with the topic of forgiveness and am much more attentive whenever I am aware of its presence in a situation, I am no longer afraid of it. I believe I get myself into situations often requiring me to accept my responsibility to request forgiveness from another. If I claim the responsibility, it is an asset in allowing me the opportunity to experience much more positive; consequently, less negative within today.

It is my belief that my Heavenly Father is totally capable of handling the vengeance aspect. He has given me the gift of not feeling the need to give that issue a second thought. So, the past is the history and today is the now and I am looking forward to the tomorrow. I now have the capacity to forgive and accept forgiveness without sensing a requirement to deny a part of me or of my life story. I know how to label my responsibility and to claim it as is required of me (quite often, I might add). I recognize I maintain the ability to thwart misguided guilt, misguided responsibility, misguided blame, and misguided claim. I also recognize I have a requirement to label situations calling for me to claim guilt, claim responsibility, and claim blame.

To accomplish God's will for me, I cannot be consumed by the past; but rather be living in this day with an open mind and my eyes looking forward and upward rather than backward.

SUPPLEMENT to FORGIVENESS

1. Do you believe it is possible for an individual to use forgiveness as a weapon? Defend your answer.

2. Do you believe it is possible to define forgiveness in a manner that produces toxicity? Defend your answer.

3. Do you believe forgiveness can be claimed as a responsibility by you unreasonably? Would the same apply to others? Defend your answers.

4. Is it possible that you have been viewing forgiveness in the same manner you did as a young child? Would it help you in any way to examine the possibility? Clearly and concretely write your definition of forgiveness. No fair using a dictionary!!!

5. If you believe forgiveness is a recurring piece in the puzzles your situations have shown you, consider a concrete goal now if you identify an unacceptable connection. In writing the goal/s, remember to honestly claim any responsibility for which you are required. Don't forget to celebrate!

FORGIVENESS ADDENDUM

If you do not believe you are yet ready to tackle this subject, I would like to commend you for having the strength to begin reading this. My prayer is that, at the close of the last page, you will be thankful you did. I think, when I was at this chapter in my initial healing process, I may have skipped it. Today, however, the subject is not as threatening as it was for many years. I feel I am in a good place with the forgiveness issue--most days. At times, however, I still struggle with the issue; and am choosing to accept that it can sometimes be the reason I need to pray that I will be able to forgive self along with others. Although, as a believer, I accept I am required to forgive, define self as a sinner and pray for forgiveness for my sins, I also believe this definition can be the hardest for <u>any</u> abuse victim to tackle, possibly dependent upon the other humans within the current environment.

When I began the ladder climb, my personal definition of forgive agreed with definitions which included not continuing to hold resentment against the 'enemy'. Have you ever seen a positive in a definition of the word 'enemy' used anyplace? Have you ever noticed that 'feelings' are often connected within the definition of forgive? If you agree with my answer of yes, then would you agree that one 'feeling' that is probably present, especially in an adult, would be anger...that alone causes me to stop and ponder. I have also been in conversations like this: (you say I need to forgive=I say what does that mean? = they say you need to pardon= I say what does pardon mean? = they answer, well, it does not mean forget... but 'forgive' = I give up). I beg of you, Helpers, to always tread extremely carefully when forgiveness is the topic being discussed as it can be extremely threatening to one of three people. And I also strongly suggest that you do what I have done and note words that are often used in conversations regarding forgiveness by studying those words in dictionaries. I always use a student dictionary when doing this regarding abuse conversations. Why? Because I have been in conversations with children regarding sexual abuse, as well as having experienced it, and I will tell you that there are extremely smart first-graders who will likely go to a dictionary to look up words being used in the definition and then look up those words! I expect another to accept, as I did, believing the self-identification like situations teach. …. Is the victim being told that he/she is required to believe that what happened is normal and acceptable?... It feels like I am a nothing. …

I remember writing a paper about this issue in graduate school and defined the victim with a self-identity as a 'non-entity'. … I was sharing my definition of self in that paper. However, I believe when a child, I would have used the word 'thing' because I knew others could see me and 'use and beat me', so they knew I was there. Please walk with caution and try to not use words you cannot readily define so that the person with whom you are conversing can understand what you are saying, particularly children. … I do have the sense that any young child who has shared with me was not near as angry as I, the adult listener by what they were stating. Consequently, my thinking is that anger may not be as big an issue for some children as are fear and confusion and much questioning regarding self. Can you agree that children are taught by familial significant others and tend to self-define using those teachings? Can you agree that the word, 'child' and the words, 'intelligence level' do not contain identical definitions in a dictionary.

Children become adults, perhaps adults who have children they then teach. How important do you think it is for anyone to identify and heal present negative effects from experiencing a past abuse? Do you think it is possible that the timing of the healing can be an important factor to consider? Do you think choices regarding the healing process made by victims in this day have the potential to affect upcoming generations? Is it possible that the helper could also affect the future of the victim in the conversation by what he/she states as well as the environment created in which the current conversation is taking place?

How many times have we said to another: "You need to forgive.", then turned, and walked away? Is it possible we were talking to a survivor of abuse who still accepts he/she is not as good as anyone else? ... I challenge you to convince me how we are, so far here, <u>not</u> telling an abuse victim: " You aren't allowed to have a feeling of anger regarding what they did to you... You are not allowed to 'pay back' in any way...You need to bury the life-story pages on which it happened (which research has reported includes burying any good memories, emotions, senses, etc. with the bad). ... Pretend it did not happen. ... Live a facade...You cannot talk about it because it makes others uncomfortable. ... It is inappropriate. ... You are a non-entity". I not only identify such comments in my childhood, but also in my recent life from fellow adults.

If you are desiring to help others with abuse issues, please consider that adults are not the only ones dealing with results of abuse in their daily lives. Also, please recognize that you will <u>never know</u> what is written on every page of another's story, neither will you obtain the ability to identify every result they have experienced... children...teens...adults...seniors. Please assume that much in every conversation. It is my experience in conversations in which I am answering questions of other helpers, that to answer a question of "why do you say that? / what is your conclusion to that? /etc.; my answer is generally another experience I have not shared. Puzzle pieces of our life stories are often interconnected, aren't they?

For me personally, standing on the Foundation, forgiveness and sin were still issues not yet studied. Generally, while on the ladder, I tended to mark those pieces of the puzzle and set them aside to address when I was stronger (or, probably, honestly, that I ignored out of fear of being back in the pit again as significant others in scenarios were periodically still in my life). That is <u>until </u>the Sunday, about 14 years after the pit experience, I heard a sermon. When returning to the church, I heard a definition of forgive that truly allowed me to take a deep breath of reassurance that I was not able to experience prior to that Sunday. The definition, as I remember it, was: "I give up **my right** to hurt you for hurting me".

Emotions (feelings) are included in any abusive situation. For me, shame, guilt, anger, and self-identification were (and still are) factors in my dealing with forgiveness. I often was questioning, do I ask for forgiveness, give forgiveness, or identify my sins. It makes total sense to me that anyone who has been abused may be dealing with the same issues and it is mandatory, in my view, for all emotions to be claimed correctly. I believe shame, guilt, and self-identification to be not only favorite weapons of Satan, but highly effective ones as they make it easy for a victim to claim unrequired negative results from abusive pasts. It is difficult to not feel shameful when one has been consistently taught, he/she is not worthy... just a 'thing'...not a person. My guess is that there is not a piece in my abusive puzzle pieces that would not relate all three issues for me when I was that victim fighting for an identification of a person like others and worth healing. When you do not believe you are as good as everyone else, they always seem happy and sure of themselves. It is not difficult to be ashamed and guilty when struggling to identify a specific sin for which to request forgiveness and only have confusion for an answer.

. However, I would not suggest spending time struggling to label sins for which one <u>may</u> be required forgiveness until after the ladder climb. I found it took practice before it became easier to identify my claiming responsibilities quickly and reasonably. My expectation of another with an abusive background who has gone through the previous chapters would be that he/she has often recognized labeled claims and responsibilities that were unrequired (which may have also brought forth anger). For me, personally, I feel it was a requirement to have that take place <u>prior</u> to dealing with forgiveness. As, for me, it was possibly the most important issue to 'get right'.

As helpers, I believe it is a requirement we realize that IF <u>we</u> choose to put forgiveness in the conversation when helping another, we are no doubt also including not only sin, but the emotive issues involved (possibly unrequired). Perhaps a helpful identification of a task for the victim to examine in the inner room prior to a discussion regarding forgiveness. Consequently, I prefer for the victim to determine when to include the forgiveness issue in the healing process. There may be some lingering issues which could hinder the forgiveness issue that still are not fully addressed and unknown.

Fellow survivor, one question in forgiveness issues that has been helpful for me to consider: Is shame a topic here or is it an issue of being shamed. Is there possibly any definition or answer or requirement, or whatever, in the scenario that has not been identified to address in thinking: shame/ashamed/shamed...which is the issue being addressed here? Scenarios can vary between these definitions, which I discovered was important for me to note and which also aided me with the forgiveness issue. I think most chapter titles could possibly affect a definition of forgiveness required within the scenarios studied in a healing process.

Helper, please take on the responsibility of asking and answering yourself these questions if you are helping another with this issue: Am I going to take the responsibility to deal with what I think about this and say what I think needs to be done? Am I going to allow the individual the right to define responsibilities and answers in the scenario in his/ her inner room? If you had this exact same experience described in the scenario given; I believe your thinking at this point, would not be written on your page with the exact wording of the one currently struggling. Why? Because you did not live *every other one* of his/her puzzle pieces. And, if you had, I still believe you would not have the exact issues defined the exact way this victim in front of you does in this conversation. Consequently, you would probably list totally different things to address.

Shame was a common negativity I labeled as experiencing on the ladder climb; and I believe it is extremely important to identify when forgiveness is the issue being addressed in examining an abusive scenario. I have reached the conclusion that any emotive results of the abuse can have a powerful effect on my personal definitions and/or conclusions, and sometimes actions in the present if I am not careful. And it makes sense to me that it may not be readily recognized in a believer when defining responsibilities in personally labeling forgiving; more so if defining self as a victim rather than survivor currently. I discovered, for me, it was pivotal to recognize <u>unrequired negatives</u> when the time came that I decided to 'take on and tackle' the forgiveness issue. But I had to be at a place where I could accept the definition of me from God to be able to define the unrequired claiming I was accepting and then choose accordingly, as well lean into the strength He gifts to take the action required to be turned into positives.

I think it is important for each one of us to recognize and respect that each individual life story is a determining factor, not only as to 'who one is today', but also how we may differ in response to the same trigger. But, when trying to help another, I believe God expects us to identify others, Including the broken, as He does: <u>equals</u>. A conversation in which forgiveness and identifying personal sin has become a topic requires me to proceed with caution because, whenever I have dealt with a negative trigger, it generally is somehow connected to an abusive puzzle piece from the past. And I have read that when memories surface, the emotions, physical, etc. come along for the ride. (My experience has also verified this.) I think you can assume, the victim sitting there talking to you now, is feeling ashamed or shamed in a conversation regarding forgiveness, or at least confused and requesting verification if he/she asked you for help. (If you are reading this to help yourself, know that today, I can tell another I am helping about a past puzzle piece of mine without experiencing the physical or emotive negativities as I expect you will also.) One gift, for which I am thankful, that the healing ladder gave me is that when past scenarios come to me in current conversations to use as examples that is most often all they are...an example of what I am saying in this conversation. One reason I say today that I am thankful for my life story.

Forgiveness and sin are tightly connected in my view. Is it possible to deal with one and not the other? I do not remember ever asking God for forgiveness for a positive! The first person I went to for help when in the pit shamed me. I never saw her again because, on the way driving back home I, for the only time in my life, seriously considered suicide. Today, if I have been triggered and am struggling with a past abusive scenario and the person with whom I am talking brings up the word forgive or sin, I will probably never call that person again for help or advice. It would also cause me to be 'guarded' whenever talking with him/her. Please give me the respect I deserve as a fellow believer, to assume that I, a believer, always identify myself as a sinner and consequently realize I am responsible, as a believer, to forgive others the same as you are. Therefore, please allow me my right to determine at what point in my healing I need to lean into forgiveness as an issue I am ready to attack (my desire is that I do the same when trying to help non-believers also). Remember, the only one who experienced each piece of this puzzle is the one sharing the story and there is not another human that identifies every puzzle piece in that person's life story.

Because I think for any believer this is one of the most important struggles, it may be a mistake to turn to this chapter first without going through the steps in each previous chapter. Practice in using the tools shortened time required with each piece I examined regarding forgiveness because one result was that I changed how I had been defining my responsibilities and claims as well as how I defined the whole puzzle piece in my hand! Consequently, I would not use the suggestions in this section before having practice with each of the prior tools that I defined as beneficial. Doing so with each puzzle piece identified, for me, personal characteristics as well as beliefs that I did not recognize I held. And it may be those characteristics that play a pivotal role in defining and dealing with forgiveness.

Now, assuming previous chapter titles have been addressed, and you define self currently as survivor rather than victim, let's continue the title of forgiveness: The other people in the pieces I examine working on forgiveness are often key. I found I had to experience the scenario 'in their shoes' also before I could effectively identify forgiveness within each individual scenario. Invariably, doing so gave me a perspective that differed from my original definitions when on the ladder defining from my stance only. Sometimes my definition of my responsibilities within the scenario changed also. However, I believe it is most effective in familial situations or perhaps a life-long friend; because it makes sense that knowing a lot about the other is a requirement as I would take on the role of the other without changing the scenario. My guess is that the piece in your hand is one that you have examined often. But, this time, do not be surprised if everything about it shifts if you choose to apply a tool which has helped me profoundly with the forgiveness issue even aiding me in my personal definition of the word forgive. Identify the individual within the scenario that is key in the forgiving. Now, you are not you but the other without changing anything else in the puzzle piece. You have taken on the other's history (their education, the things you know about them that make them who they are, etc.) and you are now that other in the same scenario. When you are ready, roll the tape and then move to the next two paragraphs prior to closing the book:

WARNING: If you experience the reactions that I have in doing this, remember that others in this past scenario are currently making choices that may differ from yours. The same applies to you. It was often difficult for me to stop, take a breath, and pray before making any sudden moves at this point. Please do that now if you are excited. Now, if this exercise has given you totally new insights, you may decide to redefine forgive in this scenario and do whatever you are required to do as your responsibility. (again...if, right now you want to call the other in this past scenario; maybe wait a couple days while praying. It may, at minimum, change what you wish to say. I have made an error by contacting and thus hurting others who were not working on this issue. Remember, we all make choices and then pay the personal consequences for the choices we make in our daily lives; and our choices vary.)

For me, the resulting insights I have learned by doing this exercise are positive rather than negative. I have also realized that, after doing this; it must be remembered that I am the only one I can change. I am the one choosing to do these exercises. I am the only one responsible to experience the consequences of my choices. My experience has been, however, that when I am successful with this exercise, my anxieties regarding forgiveness are not only definable but often dissipate as I realize forgiveness is no longer defined by me as an issue within the scenario. I reacted to the same scenario totally differently in the place of the other.

Healing from abuse is a tough road to travel and the job of a helper is a tough one. I thank God that, as a believer, He gifts me Himself, an Ally stronger than any enemy. However, we have also been given free life choices. We are not forced to choose to deal with our issues, just to experience the consequences of our choices. Abusive experiences teach many lasting (if not addressed) negativities to the victim over time. More evident, perhaps, in situations in which the abuse has been ongoing. In which case, there probably have been more negative messages given to the victim over the person's life span than positive. Research has stated that it is not uncommon, in an abusive environment, for one individual in the setting to be the target of abuse. The effects of abuse can be numerous and may be physical as well as psychological. Each person is different and has had a different whole-life story than anyone else. An important factor to remember in dealing with forgiveness of past is that the others involved in the scenario being examined may describe it differently. Consequently, I prefer, as a helper, whenever I am in a conversation with others sharing their abuse story it is important that I remember I was not the one living their life...it is their story, not mine. Therefore, I prefer, as a helper, to let the person sharing the story make all the definitions. Hopefully allowing them to guide what they will be thinking about in the inner room and how to write their personal goals regarding this forgiveness issue. I prefer not to have that responsibility. It is not my life we are talking about in a conversation in which someone has come to my door to discuss a trigger they have just experienced. And I also do not expect another I ask for help taking that responsibility away from me! (If you are my helper, and you disagree with my definition of forgiving in a scenario and feel you are required to speak; instead of telling me I am wrong, consider asking me why I define it as such and nothing else. Then I MAY think about it further.

I have been requested to give a very exact example of how to help another. A puzzle piece from my teen-age years came to my mind with the question; consequently, I have studied this piece on the ladder both as a victim and in self-counseling. This is my story...I am the only person who experienced in this scenario what I experienced. I would <u>not </u>assume another individual with a like experience would describe the negativity in the exact manner as I. I believe that one shoe <u>never</u> fits all. The definition of 'individual' <u>does not include</u> sameness to others. My goal in sharing my puzzle piece as well as my explanations include the following: Helper-- This may help you more easily gain insight into one who shares with you experiences unlike what you have experienced. Fellow victim/ survivor -- see, you are not as 'different' as you have assumed. I have been asked to keep writing because 'they don't get it'. Maybe these next pages will help 'them' get it. Fellow victim/survivor-- I know I do not have to explain it to you; but please know this: When I finish typing these addendums, I am closing these pages and will put the book back on the shelf, turn into this day assuming I will not think about it again until it may come into a conversation as an example to someone who has said something to me that brings this scenario into my mind. Then, when that person leaves, I will close the book and put it back on the shelf. Trust me, I have experienced this for the past twenty years--I do not expect to think about it again unless I need to polish the positive with it. If I can experience that, it is available to you to have a like experience; you have come so far and met so many goals.

It really is a great, huge, positivity to accomplish living life accepting self as an equal!

Leaning into the memory to re-experience it, I believe this is how I would have described it to a helper when it happened: T= teenager...

Scenario: T is sitting at the family dinner table with mother, dad, and a sibling ... Mother says to T: "Don't you love me anymore?" ... T: "Oh, mother, of course I love you" (in a snotty way).. ... Dad gets up, comes around the table, and knocks T on the floor and is kicking her, etc. When she can get up, she goes to the bathroom to lift the toilet lid and 'spit' into the toilet...she is required to flush frequently because blood is pouring from her and circulating in the toilet bowl. She is scared......

As I type this, I can sense the fear--because I was that teen, and for years this scenario was one of many included in the" forgiveness closet" in my inner room. I can tell you this much which might help you get a sense of the other in a like conversation---In this scenario, I did not feel God by me when standing at that toilet after that beating. And, let me add, that I would want to kick anyone today who tells me I 'should' have. Also, because I was a believer at the time, I felt I had sinned in the way I spoke to my mother. I thought there are some rules in the Bible about respecting one's parents. (My dad was a deacon of the church and my mother a deaconess, so I was familiar with that type of teachings in the Bible.) ... Note the helper was only told the scenario on the puzzle piece; not the information about me (T) that I just added. Consequently, the helper does not know this whole paragraph.

First, let's go back to the 'scenario'-- and what clues I've underlined and how I would define them as helpful to the listener: 1. Because she defines her response to mother as 'snotty', I assume that could be one of the reasons, or only reason, why we've got this as a 'forgiveness issue' in today's conversation (snotty is probably never a positive reference to the person using it). 2. She is the only one who goes anyplace. The assumption would probably be (and correctly) that he returns to his chair and the other two at the table stay in theirs when T goes to the bathroom---which, would probably be a rather good clue as to the life this T has in the household with all at the table. 3. She is scared (not explained specifically...but it was the blood that was scaring me...I thought I might be going to die by the toilet that night) -- that word verifies the thought at the end of 2.... There is no expectation of anyone coming to help her... would that not be a good clue as to how many times this individual has been 'misused'? When with this teen in this conversation, please treat her as an equal and only silently note your opinions; ask no questions about the scenario. Do not force her to continue reliving this scenario (or any other she shares) one fraction of a second more in her life. No matter how many specific questions you ask about the scenario itself, it will not change. But what it will do is continue to force the individual you are asking to lean into the negativity and re-experience it emotionally as well as physically.

Now, I would like to share my thoughts as I think about what I experienced in this past scenario on my puzzle piece. Although I am not that teen sitting here typing this, I can guarantee that I can identify what the victim experienced. Hopefully, it will help you help another because I can also share with you today the 'unshared' part of the story I would not have shared with a helper had one been offered when I was that high-school student. AGAIN, AS A HELPER, I WOULD ONLY NOTE THESE SILENTLY; NEVER ASKING QUESTIONS REGARDING THE SCENARIO ITSELF FORCING THE VICTIM/SURVIVOR TO RE-EXPERIENCE IT. But I assume what I underline might apply to scenarios and healing issues of others, both believers and non- believers. (I have also been asked to define the differences in my helping a non-believer vs. a believer; a hard question for me to answer because when someone comes to me for help, I do not consider that as a determining factor in how I respond). But what I typed in the following paragraph, is that which I can address regarding my past puzzle piece 64 years later:

1. Sensing the fear I felt as that teen when typing the scenario, verifies the importance of a helper to always recognize the individual sharing the abusive story is probably re-experiencing it as they are describing it to you. (As I type it on this page, I re-experience in the same manner you probably do in remembering the past scenarios you 'relive' from your past.) It helped me as a survivor to read this because it is easy to feel alone in the healing process of abuse, especially as a believer dealing with the forgiveness issue, particularly. Forgive was the most threatening word used within the Christian community to me for years. Today, it remains a word that grabs my attention in any conversation and I listen carefully to what is said next. Consequently, it is probably a good idea to give time to take a breath after someone has been sharing regarding forgiveness.

2. The Forgiveness Closet: Often when on the ladder, I labeled forgiveness as an issue in examining puzzle pieces; but did not deal with that negative because I did not feel strong enough. Consequently, I did not deal with forgiveness until I heard the phrase in the sermon: "I give up my right to hurt you for hurting me". I think another thing that helped me was that, when I was in church that Sunday, I was already getting closer to self-identifying as equal AND studying the Bible AND feeling the presence of God more consistently.

3. I have been asked if I felt God's presence when being abused. I am not comfortable asking a fellow-abuse survivor if they positively felt God with them during the abuse (or any other time); I believe it is a judgmental question, personally. If I come to you for help reliving the scenario while describing it to you and you say anything about God being there; I believe I

would immediately feel shamed because I did not ask God for forgiveness for being so terrible a person to have been punished so severely!!! But I think the answer to the question is that I never felt God's presence when in an abusive situation, not as a teen nor an adult. One tool I think I may have used during an abusive scenario was to 'go elsewhere' in my mind (non-entity thing) because I think it helped to not feel the physical pain of the abuse. You may have the opinion that not sensing God's presence is an important factor; but, if anyone ever brought it up to me, personally, I would not talk to them again because I would define them as an abuser. I think for someone else to bring it up, today, they would be judging my status as a true believer. I defined myself as a believer; and I believed I was responsible <u>always</u> to define my sin and ask God to forgive me.

4. I find the underlined statement that sin is defined as the comment to mother (not the following abuse) interesting. ... Could the helper (or the victim in the inner room) recognize some definitions already labeled by T. ... my guess is this teen <u>would not </u>have argued at the time of the beating that she did not deserve it believing she was to show respect to a parent; a rule she did not follow at the table. The helper may gain information the victim has not yet identified by noting the verbiage the victim uses in describing the scenarios. I do not know and would not ask (and am not going to stop and try to answer it now because I do not want to stay here with this memory. However, I can guarantee you I was not surprised; I doubt that I questioned at the time why it happened. I do remember being worried about was going to school with physical scars others at school would notice). The important thing to note is the T is considering forgiving as HUGE and yet VERY THREATENING, an issue that any believer probably confronts when victimized by another.

5. After all, she is in a church- family and sees the rule of forgiveness and defining sin as a rule required for a good Christian as well as possibly defining her eternity.

6. This teen's parents were leaders in the church. Which, I am sure made it harder for me (that teen) to not put them on a much higher plane than myself in God's eyes. Could this be an important consideration for the helper to quietly monitor if the family in the scenario is included within your church family? What would the cost be to this victim and, possibly the birth family, to deal with this issue openly with another in the church family?

Consequently, I believe any abuse victim who has lived in an abusive environment with believers has negativities to deal with in the healing process that are not on the list of others. I also think that believers have many added issues with which to identify and set goals around than do non-believers. I also believe this could be an issue that would prevent a person within a church body to share with others in the church body; assuming every believer has a goal to 'follow the rules' and be pleasing to God.

Another memory is coming to mind regarding a believer-victim's resulting definition of self and how it affects him/her. I am alone on the floor of the church nursery in the dark praying to God as a Jr. High/H.S. student feeling guilty (I have no idea why; I think I could not identify why at the time), but I feel a responsibility involving what I heard that happened to an older gal in the church who had been killed by a city bus. I do not remember a relationship with her. But what I do know is that I was praying to God to bring her back to life; and, if He did, I would be a missionary for the rest of my life. This memory has come to me in conversations regarding the 'rule' of claiming personal sin, guilt, responsibility, then asking for forgiveness. (All I can tell you to describe the 'why' in this scenario is that I felt her death was my fault...but I do not believe I could define why... which is why I isolated myself in the dark church nursery that night... to 'cut a deal with God' probably because of fear that God may be mad at me and send me to hell when I die.) Yes, I agree ... crazy thinking but... That is how HUGE the issue of forgiveness can be for a believer-victim experiencing and accepting the effects of a current abusive life and dealing with the issue of forgiveness. WALK CAUTIOUSLY.... PLEASE!

The self-counseling sessions I give to myself regarding my issues verify what I have read about God not changing the scenario when it comes back and emotions, feelings, shame, guilt...you name it, coming along with the memory. I used my own experiences here because I am uncomfortable answering a question asking what I would do or say to another because I have not been the one talking to the person with whom you have conversed. Here is how I examined puzzle pieces of mine: I reviewed the chapters while studying the puzzle piece in my inner room--self-identity, responsibility, claiming--seemed to be key issues to identify in these and many other scenarios...and, extremely helpful when deciding it was time to deal with forgiveness and, guess what!

One thing that comes to my mind that I think is not addressed often enough in counseling sessions (never in any of mine, nor do I remember it ever coming up in a college class) is the question that may need to be asked in a conversation: Who is it that you are required to forgive (waiting to see if self is on the list as it has been very helpful for me, when I was far enough along in the process-- not on the first rungs--to consider if I needed to forgive myself for anything at any time). I do not want to spend the time trying to count the times I, as a victim, took on unrequired responsibilities; probably any chapter title you want to choose from this book, for years... not helping my self-identity as not being an equal to another breathing entity; certainly not helping in any manner with a forgiveness issue! And, guaranteed, I do <u>not</u> stand alone!

It is easy for a victim to stay within the scenario; but it may be extremely important to remember the past cannot be changed. Another question that might be helpful to both of you (helper/survivor) is to ask: How does this story connect to the issue we were discussing? This is how I worked through my scenarios as my own counselor. I could not do it, however, until I was at the point that I was no longer self-centered and had the ability to erase me and be the others in like scenarios (their history--education/life story as I know it--age--relation to me, etcetera). I believe God is now bringing these scenarios to me to have me study them in writing this addendum to help you and me help others. But...in referencing these stories as a helper in the conversation in which the fellow believer told them (ONLY if asked to give my opinion, would I perhaps reference abusive scenarios as an example of God's bringing it for the purpose of a teaching tool for us to use somehow... something not yet identified that is connected to the story...but how?... another tool from the best Ally in the world?) But something for the victim to identify, not me as a helper...because I have not lived that life story...God is the only one with the whole picture. I think that is why various scenarios have come to me at various times. If it happens and I ask Him why, I am often amazed at the new insight that comes. Sometimes a scenario comes to mind when another is sharing with me and I have identified there is something in my page that may be of help to them gain insight into their puzzle piece. Rather than ask questions and try to provide answers for anyone asking me about their stories, I prefer to share what methods have helped me to gain insight that I cannot give another because I am not them and did not have their exact experience. I can tell you this, though, it is my experience that another will often ask me the question: "How did you deal with this?" And, when I share, I get a response of "me too"--shame, guilt, self-identification, blah, blah, blah. Consequently, I feel God tells you and me that we are not as alone nor weird as our incorrect personal identifications (and, perhaps, other humans) have defined us.

You, as a fellow-believer helper, may decide this might be a good time to quote some Scripture; and you could be right. However, I believe it is important to choose appropriately. For instance, if the woman in front of me has shared a puzzle piece of sexual abuse, I would <u>not</u> use the' forgiveness verse' referencing the harlot. Does it show the grace the Lord gives? Absolutely!!! Does it show me that Jesus identified her as an equal to any other with whom He spoke? Absolutely!!! <u>However,</u> chances are that the person to whom I am speaking would state I called her a harlot. That would have been my reaction in a conversation asking for help regarding forgiveness at an early stage in my healing process. I believe any female who has experienced sexual abuse has fought that as an appropriate inflicted self- identification. It would have been offensive to me, and I argue with anyone who says it would <u>not</u> be for another, because my helper would have just verified my self-inflicted identification of 'harlot'. I know this is hard for one who has never experienced like situations to understand; but, when I am a 'victim', telling me what I am experiencing is not required and does not help <u>if I have not asked</u>. It is difficult for me to explain why, but here is what I know:

I know, when a victim, I am not only seeing it, but I am experiencing it… emotionally, physically, psychologically, and I am believing it because 'feeling it' makes it present tense and concrete… therefore, real. Another telling me what I am feeling or experiencing is not true nor necessary or whatever; is telling me I am a non-entity because I am reacting to what I am reading on the pages of <u>my</u> Life's story. For me, and I am certain others, another telling me I am wrong about what I am experiencing is just another form of judging me and giving me another battle to win. It is also <u>definitely</u> forcing me to stay in the negativity and probably the scenario because, If I have the strength, I will argue with you rather than allowing you to negate or define <u>my</u> puzzle piece that <u>I</u> experienced on a page in <u>my</u>

life story. I am not saying, Helper, that you are wrong in an opinion you may have. But, rather, I am asking to allow the other to have control in the conversation. A requirement for me to define self as a survivor is that I readily accept a premise as true because I believe it...NOT because you believe it or declare it. We both will walk out that door and into present life after this conversation and experience consequences for choices made.

If, instead, I am encouraged to use my preferred tools in the scenario identifying responsibilities and claiming; I may be able to recognize any unrequired negativity I am experiencing. After all, if an adult is required to struggle to identify sin that he/she has committed, does it not make sense that it is a distinct possibility that something is being claimed as a responsibility that is non-existent or not required? I can guarantee you that I identify forgiving as a crippling, threatening issue for me for years. Because I believe forgiveness is so important and yet threatening, I prefer, as a helper, to not mention it until the other feels strong enough, or comfortable enough to tackle it usually by saying the word 'forgive'. However, I always expect any believer dealing with abuse is struggling with forgiveness/sin issues, probably on any given rung on the ladder climb. Therefore, I prefer to stay in present tense in conversations because the present is addressing the effects of the scenario that, hopefully, will be negated or changed from negative to positive working in one's inner room using prayer and chosen tools. Then, perhaps a discussion describing the positive results instead of the past abusive scenario!

It makes total sense to me that believers dealing with any healing process are also dealing with spiritual warfare. I believe Satan's goal for a believer would be to not heal. Consequently, I think he aims his darts to pierce deeply into my most troubling struggles because that is where I identify myself as being the most vulnerable. I am always more aware of Satan when I am questioning and confused; wondering why I cannot make 2+2=4! Consequently, if I am with a struggling survivor who I assume is generally following God on a chosen path, I <u>may</u> decide to remind him/her that the armor of God is always available and that <u>the current struggle may be</u> because <u>the survivor is doing exactly what God is directing; consequently, the current environment is the battlefield of spiritual warfare</u>. It encourages me currently when I am questioning to think of the Helmet which protects the brain. However, <u>WARNING:</u> Helper... when I was on the first rungs of the ladder and struggling to just hang on, a discussion of warfare or armor was not encouraging. However, if the other brings up the subject; the offensive armor of His Word (the Bible) and prayer is gifted to us, and standing is never required for them to be used. Our Ally is right beside us in this battle...The latter would be helpful for the victim who currently feels he/she cannot stand IF he/she has brought spiritual warfare into the conversation.

The piece of the armor of God yet to be referenced is the helmet. It makes sense to me it would be labeled as the Helmet of Salvation because God has gifted so much to us within our salvation, hasn't He? One gift is His forgiveness... given covered in red from the blood of Jesus on the cross with my sins allowing me to spend eternity in Heaven with Him. One could assume that would be enough, but God disagrees. He also provides His grace, His constant companionship allowing the child in me to close my eyes at night feeling safe to sleep soundly and awake to positivity in tomorrow, maybe even giving Him something to smile about (I hope!).

God is my constant Ally against the devil; but I, at times, have a problem with laxness allowing Satan's darts to affectively hit the targets. I believe it is well within reason, that Satan's list of targets for his darts would certainly include survivors who have abuse on past life-story pages. I readily assume an abuse victim who has spent time healing and becomes a contributing asset to the group of believers is exceedingly high on that list.

We are very good at saying: "you need to forgive" …. "you owe me an apology". I now think spiritual warfare when in a conversation regarding forgiveness with a fellow believer (but hopefully do not say it out loud if the other is struggling). As a helper talking with a fellow believer, I think the following thoughts are required of me to monitor silently: 1. Who is the enemy here...could it be Satan? 2. Are we studying identifications within definitions God provides? If that is true, am I remembering that God sees me as an equal to the other in front of me (O). Now, if I am equal to O, then O has got to be equal to me in God's eyes. So, maybe, instead of trying to figure things out now, if O has requested a discussion; it might be beneficial to see if we are on the same page with the definitions being referenced in the discussion and if they agree with God's Word. And, have the ladder steps already been addressed by O in the inner room if not in our conversations...self-talk, responsibility, claiming etc. of the negativities being labeled by O. Do I always think this is important when I am triggered with a past negative?... YES, WHY?

Because I believe Satan will ALWAYS use the most important goal and most difficult past negative to the believer in any scenario to keep him/her in the dark rather than turning to God to define God's leading in the Light. And self-identity is always a good possibility to check, for an abuse survivor, particularly if forgiveness is defined as a negativity affecting one in this current day. Because forgiveness and sin are issues believers I admire choose to self-monitor; it makes sense to me that we often have many reasons to be thankful for the helmet's protection. The helmet is referenced as the "helmet of salvation" in Ephesians 6:16. Therefore, I believe that God is also protecting our brains against the attacks of the devil. God knows how my brain works, and He protected me with His gift of the helmet throughout all the years I was fighting Him, because He was with me and patiently waiting. I believe the helmet of salvation helps us to reason in drawing conclusions we make allowing us the ability to stay on the path and follow His leading.

Let me tell you something...I FIRMLY BELIEVE my God knows me better than anyone, including me, and that He cares for me as no one else in my life ever has! And guess what...He feels the same way about you if you have chosen to be one of His believers.

Do you agree that it is good to choose to use our life-story scenarios in addition to our brains he has protected with a helmet to make our decisions about how we are going to turn negatives into positives in this day? He gave us free will; how soon and how often are we going to choose to follow His Word? You can use your free will to make your decisions.

Because I always think about the definition of forgiveness in the sermon, I use that: "I give up my right to hurt you for hurting me". The word that jumped out at me was 'right'. "Who said that? They must have been abused!". I reacted in this manner: 1. If I have the right to hurt back, then I must have <u>not</u> deserved it...erase trying to define my sin that caused the abuse. 2. If I have the right to hurt back, then the abuser must not be someone God is going to force me to be around… I can choose to <u>not</u> be in a relationship with the one who hurt me without God punishing me. 3. If I have the right to hurt back, then God must not agree that the abuser is more important than I… God sees me as equal with same rights as others, rather an identification as non-entity. 4. If I have the right to hurt back, then, perhaps I can close the past pages with scenarios I cannot change. 5. If I have the right to hurt back, Perhaps I can use the gifts God protects with the Helmet of Salvation by making a change for me to <u>accept and apply</u> HIS definitions of the abuse and of me deleting the teaching included in those past abusive scenarios.

Is there ever a time in the forgiveness issue in which you believe it may be appropriate to consider forgiving self? The more I think about forgiveness of self, the more I feel it could possibly be an extremely important concept for anyone to examine. Do you think it is possible that we could, today, be making inappropriate choices in our lives because we are continuing a behavior or making decisions that, in the present are not necessary? Is it possible that we felt required in our past to protect self in some manner that is not necessary in the present, but we are continuing the behavior, unknowingly in a negative fashion or with negative results; and, if so, then do not my current requirements need to be correctly identified? It makes sense to me that such a circumstance could be a possible answer to a lingering unanswered question or an identified negativity in the present for which I need not be responsible. I believe Satan uses his darts to try to keep me to act in the present according to the requirements and definitions in abusive past scenarios. If so, and not recognized by me; surely, that may cause me to detour from the path following God's will today.

When one is alone and working on healing in the inner room … no facade, right? The following quote In the Bible's Book of Romans was helpful and still is today. Paul wrote this in his letter to the church in Rome which *"focuses on salvation as a gift from God, through grace, by the blood of Christ Jesus"*(NIV p.1220): *"Do not repay anyone evil for evil. Be careful to do what is right in the eyes of everyone. If it is possible, as far as it depends on you, live at peace with everyone. Do not take revenge, my dear friends, but leave room for God's wrath, for it is written: 'It is mine to avenge; I will repay, says the Lord'"*(Romans 12:17-19 NIV p1232). When I put this verse alongside the sermon quote, a new concept began to emerge. I began to believe that God 'got it'. I believe I began to 'get it' when I connected me closer to the cross. Could it be possible that one reason Jesus CHOSE to go to the cross was to 'get' us? Please take note of the first four words in Romans 12:18: *"If it is possible"* (I notice the word "if" is forced to be capitalized). Yes, Jesus chose to come to earth and experience it for himself accepting the payment of the cross for the choice. But these four words would not be on the page from one who does not 'get it'. In my opinion, this is a pivotal message Jesus gifted for ones who are struggling to not believe the teachings of abuse. But, rather to accept and apply the teachings of healing from abuse I now define in the Bible. He CHOSE to come and pay the penalties for our sins; allowing you and me to have these messages for support in our most difficult battles.

I stopped wasting time thinking I could not be a good Christian until I labeled my sin within the abuse and asked for forgiveness; but, rather, I started labeling what I felt God was directing in my life.

In the process, I found I was forgiving myself for wasting so much time because if I am good enough for Him to be angry and punish for abuse towards me, and He was with me throughout it all; then I will choose to ask Him to negate the negativity of the abuse allowing me to turn to Him for definitions, insights, answers, and guidance. I was then able to polish identified positives as He was not requiring me to keep the abusers in my life. I began to label the gifts He gives in our salvation as well as recognize experiencing them in my daily life. His presence became more and more concrete to me and the shame, guilt, anger was dissipating. I was living in an area with God and dogs in which I may not see another human (but lots of animals), if I did not leave the property. And guess what, I could go to sleep at night without experiencing triggers, nightmares, or fear!

"For I am convinced that neither death nor life, neither angels nor demons, neither the present nor the future, nor any powers, neither height nor depth, nor anything else in all creation, will be able to separate us from the love of God that is in Jesus our Lord."

(Romans 8:38-39 NIV p1228)

LIVING A FAÇADE

Facade is an interesting word to me. It brings to one's consciousness a sense of mystery, misleading's, darkness, and a whole gamut of emotions ... but, mostly, it brings an awareness of secrets. When I have defined myself in a circumstance in which I feel dishonesty is required of me, answering the following question has been helpful before taking an action:

> "In what way is living this facade aiding me
> in accomplishing my current goals?"

Taking such a step before leaning into the superficial and involving oneself in the situation may allow one to be in fewer such scenarios. Are there times when one may be in a position in which it is best for all involved <u>not</u> to immediately answer? Perhaps an example may be when dealing with a child who is asking the tough questions. Some conversations may be best shared only when people have reached the appropriate maturity level. The question, perhaps to ask oneself, however, might be: Is not sharing a requested secret lying? Perhaps requesting time to think about it would be an acceptable immediate response to the question.

If one is struggling with living a facade, I would suppose that he/she may be in the place I have been when dealing with this issue. I believe it is possible that, in my life at times, I was living a facade without labeling it. However, there were situations in which I was consciously aware of labeling it; oftentimes wishing I were not in a circumstance causing me to consider such a behavior. I, personally, have been in situations in which I felt I was living a facade and not treating myself in a healthy manner; I felt I was living a lie. There may be pertinent questions and thoughts requiring examination, possibly more than are recognized here. It is probable these vary with the situation as well as with the individual. It is also probable that the degree of pertinency shifts at various times within the same given situation.

I think it is possible that I felt required to choose living a facade in the early stages of my healing process before I had taken time to identify and use the tools to gain understanding of situations. Perhaps the more information one is gaining and understanding, and the more one is identifying the pieces fitting into the whole picture, the less one feels the need to live a facade.

Currently, I am often able to label such shifts as signs of healing presenting a cause for celebration. I am now aware that when I find myself in situations in which I would probably have chosen to put on a facade in the past; I make choices which feel healthier today. Sometimes I avoid the situation entirely. I find it encouraging to celebrate any positive shift within me allowing an opportunity to stay on the desired path leading to my defined goals.

Whatever the result of the examination as to living a facade, I believe valuable lessons in aiding an individual towards becoming the person he/she desires to be will be presented.

Why would a person consciously make the choice to live a facade; and, by doing so, include such an act within a layer in one's life story? Reasons may involve the following:

To protect one's job

To gain/maintain acceptance

To protect one's position in a group

To continue/prevent following expectations

To protect one's visible emotional wholeness

To avoid judgement

To maintain the facade

To Protect One's Job:

Does not this topic contain unique characteristics? Although I believe this topic is the most difficult in the list and, at times, certainly becomes entangled with any or all others in the list, it also may be the hardest in which to be honest with oneself. Perhaps because in most cases, at least with people in my environment, one's livelihood is dependent upon one's job. Consequently, my guess is that many of us are in a group of people who have, at some point, seriously struggled with the issue of the appropriateness of job choice. Perhaps living a facade in some situations is the most appropriate course of action.

Is it not possible for one to be in a situation, be it professional or social, in which the only result of honestly and openly sharing would be properly identified as unprofessional and/or inappropriate? When another is paying me, do I not have responsibilities to that individual or company? Is not a valid expectation that, as an employee, I follow the rules meeting the expectations to the best of my ability? Should I not expect to experience consequences for my behavior on the job site? Would it not follow that each of us has a responsibility to deal with our layers/secrets in a respectful manner?

Perhaps one aspect of living a healthy life may always include keeping one's goals in mind in every situation. The big picture, as well as how the current pieces will fit into it, also might be a helpful examination to consider. In so doing, one may cause any current decision to seem a little lighter. For some of us, in a situation in which one is grappling with the choice of living a facade on the job site, perhaps asking oneself if doing so would negatively affect the achievement of one's personal goals before taking another action may simplify and quicken the whole process making the next step much easier to identify.

To gain/maintain acceptance from others

To protect one's position in a group

To continue/prevent following expectations

An interesting observation to consider in the concept of living a facade is that one probably only uses this tool when other people are involved. When one is alone, why bother? After all, can one hide secrets from God? In my opinion no; only, maybe, people. Therefore, the others, in a situation, apparently need to be considered. Identifying all the players, including myself, and defining the roles of each, especially mine; may make the job of gaining an acceptable insight obtainable, enabling one to identify group dynamics.

When one is in a circumstance in which members, title, location, or the description of a group is important to an individual; the perceived opinion that the group members hold for him/her may have a deciding impact in the choice to live a facade when with that given group.

I believe I live in a society in which the group called family is considered in a unique manner compared to other groups; a concept not considered by me until I experienced the healing ladder. In my opinion, if one considers the familial situations within his/her life story among the most toxic, the effects of the healing-process steps can be profound. If the situation being examined involves the family group; the victim's support may shift, albeit unconsciously. Is it possible that if one's perpetrator is a parent, the responsibility of the victim is defined differently than if the perpetrator is an associate or a stranger? Is it possible that the victim as well as others; possibly for instance the support group, unconsciously accept the premise without defining it that the victim's responsibility or actions in a situation vary according to the definition of the perpetrator/s? After all, I have celebrated Father's Day and Mother's Day, but not Neighbor's Day; without a thought of putting such scenarios within this life-story. Is it possible that gaining or maintaining acceptance from others in one's family group is, consciously or unconsciously, more important than any other group in one's life? It may be an important concept for all of us to consider...certainly, perhaps at minimum, offering an argument for forcing an individual to live a facade.

When one is on the healing ladder, the opinions of others have a definite impact, negative as well as positive. When I am very certain that the decisions and actions which I accept in my daily life are right and keeping me on the path to achieve my end goals, I have no need to go back to the healing ladder for processing. But, when on the healing ladder, the opinion of others, particularly of those I consider in my support group, affect me more profoundly. Generally, I personally have discovered, that experiencing a negative trigger in the present day is what may precipitate a turn to the ladder steps.

Is it possible, however, that an opinion of another could be extremely difficult to identify? For an example, have you ever experienced an inexplicable sense of discomfort from another when in his/her presence? Obviously, there are probably many explanations for such a scenario; however, the following possibilities may be worth a glance: Could it be possible that something about me triggers something within the other, perhaps a characteristic I have? Perhaps I have shared a layer of my story that triggers an experience of yours that you have yet to identify or are trying to stuff or hide. Is it possible that some are so uncomfortable with another's life story that they are uncomfortable simply being in his/her presence? My experience verifies this may be a situation one who is struggling and sharing, possibly when within a group, may experience. I believe placement on the healing ladder may determine the explanation of such a scenario by the victim/survivor.

Sometimes, the explanation of a discomfort is much more obvious. A personal story comes to mind as I write this. I was working in a back office in a downtown setting when a burn victim was hired. It was difficult for me to look at her initially as she was so terribly scarred. However, after we had become friends spending many lunch hours shopping through the aisles of the downtown stores, I did not realize I no longer saw her scars. I received a phone call one evening from another friend who had come up to us while shopping and I had introduced them. My phone caller was asking what had happened to my friend. My response was, "What are you talking about?". I did not realize at that moment what a valuable lesson I had just been taught.

Sometimes shunning is the result of something obvious. Sometimes, shunning may be the result of an issue not previously known such as openly shared confidences, perhaps a life-story layer, which just happens to trigger another to think about a likeness in his/her story which is uncomfortable or possibly which he/she is struggling to keep hidden from others and/or self. Consequently, using tools to identify and examine the situation and to define puzzle pieces can be helpful in making healthier decisions regarding the possibility of staying in a situation and living a facade.

Is it possible that anytime a group is formed, rules or certain behavioral considerations may be implied or, perhaps, expected? I, personally, have labeled such as the source of my discomfort in some situations. Within groups with which I am familiar, such expectations range from formal dress for participation in rituals using formal-memorized text, to sharing what was written in a workbook accompanying a defined study. It seems to me, perhaps a clear understanding of the purpose of a group could be advantageous in one's decision as to personal involvement. Sometimes, when I questioned, and yet continued in the group, I felt it ended as a positive. However, at times, the group experience played a role in my slipping down the healing ladder, particularly if my staying in the group required living a facade.

Another scenario may be that one is in a situation in which the individual does not know members of the group, nor will he/she ever see them again...to live a facade may not be an issue in any manner. Is it possible, if the group holds no level of importance to the person, it is not worth the effort for him/her to live any type of a facade to protect a position nor to gain or maintain acceptance from others; nor, possibly, to follow any rules or expectations of the group? In fact, he/she may devise behaviors that would aid in leaving a group to which the individual no longer declares allegiance or no longer feels an obligation. Such a thought raises a pertinent question possibly often ignored: "Why did I initially desire to be a member of this group?"

If one is uncomfortable living a facade, an honest, personal examination may reveal interesting and helpful information. I can identify situations in which such a process has resulted in my withdrawing from a given situation or choosing not to join a particular group. In some situations, it has been helpful for me to examine if the results of the involvement would affect my achievement of personal goals. Such an examination has often aided me in reaching a quick and healthy decision.

To protect one's visible emotional wholeness

To avoid judgement

To maintain the facade

When one is not in a place of emotional wholeness, I believe it may be a common practice to choose to live a facade to hide the fact from others, particularly in certain situations or groups. Perhaps if one is on the healing ladder and others in the scenario are not; any toxic behavior may increase, adding burdens to the individual who is struggling to change. Whatever the situation, should one choose to live a facade, would one be also choosing a behavior counterproductive to emotional wholeness? There have been times in my life when I have consciously chosen to live a facade in a situation. Many times, I could label the choice as a possible avoidance of judgement from others and/or avoidance of guilt. Sometimes I have chosen such a path when the expected judgement of others aligned with the judgement which I was putting upon myself.

There have also been times in my life in which I have avoided being in situations because I recognized I would not be able to maintain living the facade required to project visible emotional wholeness. Generally, particularly when feeling somewhat vulnerable, it seems the group with which I am most comfortable without a facade is one in which I believe my position, acceptance, judgement, and honesty is not dependent upon me monitoring my verbiage, actions, and thoughts if I remain respectful and accept my responsibilities.

Is it possible that we oftentimes do not recognize the role we allow our secrets or our past life story to play in our daily lives? Do we ever give the control of our lives as well as how we live them, to others without realizing it? Do we unconsciously give our responsibility to others; or perhaps, do we consciously do so in the struggle to keep our secrets and live a facade when with them? At this point, perhaps the pertinent question becomes: "How does one prevent secrets or the past life story from keeping him/her imprisoned in negativity?"

To answer the last posed question probably would require an honest examination of the reasons for burying secrets involved in assigning oneself to live a facade in a situation. My personal belief is that, because God knows everything about us already; one only has the choice to keep secrets from other individuals, maybe! I question, for instance, how often our secrets are recognized by others in our environment without our knowledge.

It is also possible to be in a situation in which one is extremely confused and unable to answer unspoken questions, desperately trying to live a facade while struggling to maintain a perceived, albeit misjudged, opinion of others. At the same time, the others are aware of secrets in the situation that the individual is not. Such a situation presents an extremely obscure, toxic picture and one that presents a challenge in the healing process.

Sometimes, such as in the above situation, it is helpful when peeling the layers of one's life story, to back away and observe the big picture. If one accepts the possibility that the keeping of a secret by not acknowledging its existence is possibly preventing the healing of an individual; then, it seems to me that the bigger picture needs to be examined. Is it possible that my opinion of others in my environment will play a pivotal role in my choice to keep or to share a secret and/or seek support from them, or, even possibly to stay in the given situation? Is it possible that unknown secrets to me are causing me to misinterpret the big picture? If the big picture is obscure, perhaps I need to examine situations allowing me to identify hints as to the reasons for the obscurities.

My life experiences have taught me that in situations in which I cannot identify the big picture, the possibility exists that I do not have all the pieces. If this is the conclusion I draw, the job is then to discover missing pieces. In such a circumstance, one is possibly in a situation in which secrets and lies are swirling all around that are profoundly affecting the person, even though he/she is oblivious to them. In such situations, it may be vitally important to verify if you are the only adult in your life for whom you have control and/or responsibility. Honesty to oneself is a prerequisite in the healing process. It may be possible that one must accept as fact that there will always be unidentifiable puzzle pieces and some puzzles may never be completely answered.

Consciously choosing to remain in toxicity for years has resulted in, perhaps, years of my life struggling in the healing process. Time which would not have been necessary, had I asked myself years earlier: "Why am I consciously choosing to continue in the same toxic behavior over time?". I have reached this conclusion because I assume, in my case, toxicity is hidden in any scenario in which I feel obligated to live a facade over time; and, obviously, I am consciously choosing to be involved in it if I am continuing the behavior.

The questions this concept requires are many and oftentimes quite complicated if one is desiring to heal and is listing and defining the concrete steps and changes necessary to reach a desired and defined goal.

Usually, I personally have discovered that when I chose to stay in a situation requiring me to live a facade, I was also on an undetected detour from the path on which I would have been following God's lead...now for me, a continual life's goal; too often not considered by me, however!

Is it possible that the scariest circumstances in our lives may offer the most fulfilling rewards? Could it also be possible that these situations are the ones to which we will someday recall with a smile recognizing that they were the times in which we practiced our faith allowing us to be walking much closer to God?

It helps me to remember God is my one constant Ally; the One who knows me better than any human. It is when I feel unsure and hesitant that I am in danger of making dangerous choices. And, turning to Him would be a safe choice; He is <u>always</u> available. So why would one turn away from Him instead of towards Him? I am the one who pays all the consequences for my life choices. I have decided in my life, to strive to achieve one consistent goal each day... turn to my constant Ally and follow His leading because the One that is always available is the only One that knows me better than even I. I have experienced that, when I accomplish this goal, I also may have unexpected verifications from fellow humans who, unknowingly, contact me providing concrete messages indicating I am successful in following His lead.

SUPPLEMENT to LIVING A FACADE

1. As with any puzzle piece you have identified, I suggest that, if you have discovered you are living a facade in a current situation, ask yourself honestly if doing so is creating negativity for you in some manner. If so, define the negatives and decide: ok, or not ok?

2. Is Living a Facade in this current situation presenting an obstacle in the achievement of your goal? Answer and decide: ok, or not ok?

3. Determine if you are going to continue to live the facade or not, your choice and your consequences. You may decide that it is ok for now; but not forever, as I did in certain situations.

4. You may want to monitor if there may be another in your life with whom you feel required to live a facade. If so, label responsibility and claiming, then use your tools and ask yourself honestly if your behavior is hurting either of you in any way: ok, or not ok?

5. Be prepared to discover that you have been living a facade with another and not identified that you were doing it.

LIVING-A-FACADE ADDENDUM

There may be periods in one's life in which living a facade is a requirement. One may be responsible to a child or to another hurting in some manner and requiring the availability of someone stronger to lean on. I have friends currently choosing to 'give up' their personal lives for the time required to support significant others in the closing of the last chapter of their lives. I listen and watch them experience the frustration and pain they are choosing to experience. They daily sacrifice to make the other comfortable and pain free as he/she slips away at times perhaps not identifying the provider. I cannot relate to the frustration of these friends, mustering all the strength they believe they have left, as they lean into the facade they are utilizing when turning to 'authorities' for instructions to continue their chosen current path.

However, when they share with me, I do not believe they are looking for instructions. I do not currently recognize the person in the conversations as one of the strongest people in my life. I recognize one who is having trouble standing and questioning self continually; someone who needs an opportunity in which to be open, honest, and 'let it all out' screaming, crying; whatever helps, before turning back into the current chosen situation. I have no reason to assume I would have ever described these friends as 'victim', and do not now; however, I pray that I respect them in our current conversations. Because I want to help; it is extremely hard just to listen; but easy for me to admire who they are and to pray for them to recognize the strength available to them.

Could it be possible that the strongest, wisest, most capable of us may be in a situation-- broken-- feeling matched, at some point, to each description given to a 'victim' in this book; however, I do not define these people as 'victims', but strong, giving, caring...ones I personally admire. I do not believe abuse is a requirement for one to be hurting with a current, if not low at least 'extremely shaky', self-concept... questioning responsibilities, guilt, and aloneness...

required to put on a facade to appear 'capable' as others generally would describe; and experiencing the need for a concrete other to just be there and listen...no instructions, no judgements, no questions requiring answers.

My desire is that when these others turn towards me, they will be provided a safe (no facade of any kind required) and confidential place to do what is required to gain the ability to take a very deep breath before putting on the façade and again turning to others for instructions to help another. I admire these people and I always learn from them. I believe there are available positives daily if one is willing to look beyond self and learn from others. I know this much for sure: these friends provide many examples for me to follow God, listen and encourage and to grow in my daily walk. If I do, I will be closer to the person He wishes me to be.

ISSUES WITH OTHERS

Perhaps in examining your life-story layers in the preceding sections, you were able to discover many interesting things about yourself; some which you label as helping you to create positive in today's page and some not. The latter may influence issues with others more than you have recognized. The healing-ladder experience has probably forced you to realize it is not realistic to change life-long beliefs or actions overnight. You may currently be practicing changes within you allowing you to feel better about yourself and your current life-story layer. Our present dealings with others in our lives provide an excellent opportunity for us to monitor our successes in positive changes.

Because we are in an environment in which people are living longer; you may be currently, at times, with the same people present and perhaps in some of the same situations that formed your long-standing beliefs and actions. If this is the case, do you need to label possible affects you may be allowing to enter into this day? I find that the effects are more evident within my life-long group of individuals, probably because the emotions within me are heightened, an issue you may have recognized also. But is it possible that you sometimes allow any negativity you are working on changing, to bleed into current situations with others? Perhaps the current incident has triggered something within you that you have not labeled.

Remember, you have more choices now that you have additional tools and, possibly, many new scenarios with different people on the page in which you are living today. You cannot change the past; but you may make different choices or be practicing changes within you allowing you to have more positive in today's life-story page. For instance, look at the recurring issues you have found; especially the ones which you have often used as a misguided self-inflicted weapon. Accept responsibilities required of you; but do not claim the responsibilities of others! You know all of this; I am only reminding you as we talk about issues with others in our daily walks. I know me and I recognize that today, sometimes, I still forget these important insights; I allow my emotions to over-ride all else. The latter situation, by the way, may be a requirement to set the timer for a five-minute pity party. Then, when that is over, I would tend to think much more clearly.

I doubt I stand alone as one who has been in situations with other adults and felt the need to protect myself in some fashion. Have you ever been in a situation in which you felt required to have contact with someone and yet sensed that it may become a struggle to protect self while, at the same time, reflect the person you profess to be? Too often, at the conclusion of such a scenario, the consequences of my personal choices forced me to conclude that I wish I could have defined myself as having been a true example of who I desire to be.

Perhaps the ease with which we protect self is somewhat dependent upon our perception of the others in the scenario. Does it make a difference if the other is a valued friend, a family member, an acquaintance, a fellow-group member, a stranger? Does our acceptance of certain rules possibly affect our view or relationship with another? Does each person within the given circumstance have equal responsibilities, or do the 'rules' change according to the definition of the individual?

Do the same suppositions apply to each equally regarding concepts such as respect, responsibility, demands, commonly accepted group beliefs and/or expectations? Perhaps identification of such applications within the given situation before one takes an action may be appropriate. Taking a deep breath and a quick overall view of the situation may be a wise first step; you could possibly be surprised at your findings.

Are you required to maintain an ongoing relationship with one another; if so, by whose rules? Is it possible that the responsibilities of those within the scenario differ? Are there any responsibilities required to be shared equally within the situation? Are there perhaps expectations within the situation with which you are uncomfortable that you are not identifying? Is it possible that each of these questions would potentially have an impact upon any decision one might make or in defining a comfort zone? Are you required to make this decision right now, or could another meeting be scheduled to allow you time to evaluate?

Does a perceived threat always exist when one feels the need to protect self? If one feels the need to protect self, would the identification as to why be appropriate? Do you feel wronged by another in some way; if so, would a sense of guilt be appropriate? If you recognize you have wronged another, would a sense of guilt be appropriate? If you have identified an issue that you have consistently claimed within a scenario in the past; has it been beneficial to recognize...why? In reacting from a source of guilt, is it possible that you may be claiming misguided guilt; if so, could it be possible in this current situation, for you to use the guilt as a self-inflicted weapon; a weapon towards the other, perhaps? Could claiming of guilt, or any other identified concept you have labeled as an issue, reflect your perception of the other/s within the scenario? Is it possible that your opinion of the other/s or, perhaps of any applicable 'rules', play a role in any alignment of the concept of forgiveness within the puzzle? If you feel vulnerable, try to identify the threat. Sometimes, I have discovered the threat is my view or definition of certain concepts I believe apply to the situation or, sometimes what I fear are the definitions that the other/s are using within this current situation.

A discovery I made while on the healing ladder was that my self-definition at times had an impact on the scenario's development with long-standing others. I labeled myself in comparison to all others which, in turn, determined my behavior. I was surprised to discover I not only subconsciously applied long-standing beliefs when experiencing past life-story scenarios, but I was currently still doing so. I realized that I did not believe the beliefs I was acting on. If you are not able to gain a clear understanding of a relationship with another; you, too, may gain valuable insight by examining just you and how you honestly compare yourself with certain/all others and the rules you assign yourself to follow or, are following habitually. You may decide to examine certain layers of your book for help or verification. Then perhaps you will be able to label what is acceptable to you and define goals for any changes within you that you deem necessary. Do not forget to celebrate!

If I believe I am the only one for whom I am responsible in the given situation as well as the only one I can control; then is the continual use of verbiage such as "he/she/they did____" productive? Could it be possible that the time span and the extent of continuing damage are in the control of the individual in his/her own individual life? Could it be possible that the end results may vary widely between the individuals involved in this scenario?

What significance should you assign to your life goals within the examination of the current situation? Under what circumstances is it healthy to transfer control regarding the attainment of your goals to another in this, or any other, puzzle?

I do not know about you; but I have been in situations with others in which I felt the situation was controlling my life. I was not eating nor sleeping properly, I struggled to concentrate in meeting daily expectations. I was unable to prevent my thoughts regarding the situation from clouding daily requirements allowing me to achieve my life goals. If one has reached this point in the relationship, would it not be appropriate to accept the possibility that control regarding the attainment of personal goals has been transferred to another?

Who is the one most capable of defining your puzzle pieces? Who is the one experiencing the results of your exposure to the given situation? Who is the one most capable of answering your questions?

Who is the one most capable of defining the steps you should take to allow you to get back on the path leading to the attainment of your personal life goals?

In practicing the steps which you have defined as helpful for you, this situation may be used to provide further insight. A common problem for me that continues to rear its ugly head in situations with certain others is that I react emotionally instead of cognitively. When this happens to me, I have discovered that if I set the timer for a five-minute pity party, then take a deep breath before re-examining the picture, I tend to act more appropriately and positively. If you discover this helps you also, do it, and then try to look at the following concepts without emotion.

Which of my goals are at risk

I am the only one I can control

Am I claiming MY correct responsibilities

Remember, if this current situation is involving your group or person that is the hardest for you, the decisions you reach could be the hardest to follow; however, may bring the highest of rewards to you. You probably have also recognized by now that it takes a while in the healing process to have experienced the personal rewards, but remember this: If the goal is to see the view from the top of the mountain, or the healing ladder, and you decide after a couple slips that you are going to stop the process and go back: you have also decided you may never stand at the top to get that view. The older you get, the more energy it takes on the climb, trust me, I know. If you gave up ten years ago and now, ten years later, decide to get back at it; you lost ten years of that view from the top.

In examining the various pictures in your life story, it is important to remember that <u>you</u> are doing it. The others in your pictures are not you. Remember, your life story is yours and theirs' is theirs'; consequently, is it healthy to assume that someone else is going to react in a situation as you do?

If one of the individuals in this current picture is someone important in your personal life story and you know a lot about his/

her life story, maybe it would be helpful if you try to 'step into his/her shoes' and see this situation from his/her point of view instead of yours. Become an actor playing this person in this exercise. You are now playing the role of this person in the puzzle you are examining. This only worked for me when the other was a person with whom I had shared much of my life, or someone I knew well. But the results of the exercise were positive for me; not easy, not warm and fuzzy, but positive because of the clarity it brought. Did it cause the picture to bring smiles? No. Did it cause us all to love each other bunches, giving each other hugs and kisses? No. Then, why positive? Because it brought me understanding as an answer to many of my whys. It did not make anything ok, just understandable. I 'got it', it makes sense now. So, the positive I define is that I am now able to close the book and put it on the shelf and turn and walk into today back on the path to my life goal of trying to fulfill my purpose. I cannot change nor control the past; but that chapter is in the book I closed for now. I am writing a new chapter this day and the personal choices I make will determine the consequences I will pay as a result. How the other people in that past situation write today's chapter in their books is their choice.

The time may come when you ask yourself the question: Is it possible for me to remain in this relationship and be in alignment with my desired definition of self?

It may not yet be the time for you to examine that question, only you know enough to be able to answer. When significant others are involved in a puzzle I am examining; I have discovered, in an on-going situation which does not seem to change no matter what I try, it helps to look at these three concepts:

1. If it remains as it is today for years, I will be ok because....
2. I need to make some changes for this to be ok for me; but I am not ready yet. I will set this on a back burner for now.
3. This is not ok. This is not going to be ok because no matter what I do, I will not be without a threat in this relationship.

For the first time, I am convinced the threat to me is too great. Now, today, I make a difficult decision which I can revisit if or when something shifts that would allow me to be in a safe position.

Your story…
Your decision…
Your consequence to pay…

SUPPLEMENT to ISSUES WITH OTHERS

1. If you find yourself in a situation in which you have identified that you feel required to protect self and have singled out one individual in the scenario who may be the issue; is it possible that, if you change your approach with that one individual, today's picture would become acceptable?

2. Has the issue you have identified in this current scenario been frequently labeled in other puzzles you have examined? If so, would the information discovered in those situations also apply to this current situation?

3. If you are recognizing recurring issues, you may define changes in you that you want to start working on as immediate concrete goals. Perhaps, the recurring activity has been an unrecognized negativity within you that you can easily change now.

4. Is it possible that you are still living under your childhood acceptance of rules without recognizing it? My experience is that childhood rules may include definitions of others such as a policeman, doctor, minister, principal who may be in your situations now that you are an adult. Be prepared to be surprised in examining these possibilities!

5. Are you remembering to always determine in any puzzle you are examining, if you claim anything misguided; or giving your responsibility, or control of you to another?

6. Are you remembering to always and honestly label and claim any responsibilities that are yours?

ISSUES-WITH-OTHERS ADDENDUM

By the time I reached this ladder rung, I recognized that I had been living with an unrecognized self-definition from the abuse rather than from God's definition of me. I was also not describing God in the way I now believe the Bible teaches, but from the abuse-teaching that described God as always watching me to punish. Therefore, I certainly would not be turning to God's Word and church family for answers. Consequently, my life continued as existing, rather than living, because of the choices I made. The abuse throughout those years between High School and the funeral-casket experience was defined by others. I was not correctly defining abusive situations because I was no longer being physically beaten nor tied up in a closet. I was living my new life being 'successful': college degrees, nice home, cars, formals, etc. etc.; but when I went to my 'inner room', I had tons of unanswered questions and confusions. My 'successful life' continued by living a facade when I was with others or at work. It also enabled me to find the strength to get a divorce, after twenty- five years, knowing the Bible told me I had reason.

My current self-diagnosis is that, throughout those thirty years, not only was I continuing to live an abusive life; I was one of the main contributors of my abuse to me. It was the funeral-casket experience that 'threw me into the pit'; forcing me to immediately seek outside help for the first time in my life.

Helper, you could be dealing with one who is at this stage without you knowing all the information. But, as a believer he/she recognizes the need to forgive as did I. And I can guarantee you that I am not the only one who has silently defined forgiveness as an insurmountable stumbling block to feeling 'healed and worthy and equal'. After all, if your self-identity tells you that all negativity is your fault, therefore you deserve to be punished; then, you have a lot of sins to identify. But, what if you cannot, because it just is not making any sense? How can the requirements be met if you are unable to label that for which you are required to be forgiven? Each one of us may experience an unexpected trigger and find ourselves in a situation in which we feel broken and feel the need to turn to another. God defines His followers as equals. Wouldn't it be great if you and I as fellow believers had the ability to consistently follow that example?

Consider the advantages of negating the current negativity of the abuse, rather than using available strength to bury personal history when with others to feel an equal per their standards. Isn't it interesting that I only consider living a facade when with others? As a believer, I realize I am wasting my time playing that game with my Heavenly Father. Besides, it is not necessary. He already sees me as equal to all others because of the gift Jesus gave me on the cross. Consequently, I am accepted, and respected by His grace given within my salvation just as I am. And the Bible states He will handle the revenge to the perpetrators; another gift given by His grace allowing me to 'give up my right to hurt others for hurting me'. It allows me to close those pages of my life story and put the book on the shelf. I am then able to turn into today knowing He is my constant Ally rather than punisher. I have noticed that when I believe I am walking on a path following His leading, the power of fellow humans to cast negativity into this day is greatly diminished. I cannot remember when I last had a pity party...it has been too many years ago and I cannot tell you why I last set the timer for one. I can tell you, however, that during times I have struggled to agree with His definitions of me, He has sent concrete others who define me as an equal to provide the concrete I need to regain my alignment with Him.

However, in all honesty, my personal experience is that today's pages are more apt to be encouraging to me when I do not have contact with ones included in past 'negative-puzzle scenarios'. If you can agree with this premise, here is my current stance regarding helpful thinking I use personally which has helped me to be more relaxed when in contact with others involved in past negativities. Examine why is it so difficult to accept the fact we are each unique, yet equal individuals? Is it possible that the manner with which we, individually and initially, reacted and defined past negative situations... at the time it was experienced... is important to consider? Now, include the individual decisions each has followed regarding the shared incident until today...we have led different lives in the interval...each made decisions daily; consequently. also experiencing the results of same. Is it possible we ... or only one of us ... respond differently to the trigger of that shared scenario at this moment because of those personal decisions? What impact would these identified results have at this moment as we are face to face in a new scenario? How are each of us defining 'different' at this moment... does the definition of 'different' include right or wrong, or just not identical.

We are all going to have struggles; some which make us stronger and wiser. We are not required to feel comfortable and abundantly love each other preferring the constant companionship of each individual with whom we come into contact throughout our lives. I believe some of our life stories alone cause others to be uncomfortable with us. Not everyone makes like choices. In Romans, Paul states that we are to live at peace....as much as is possible. Thus, giving us the gift to turn and follow the path on which God is leading us. Which tells us not all others in our lives are going to be on the whole trip with us. We may never have the answers to all our questions; for which I, personally am thankful. He is the One with the answers and knowledge necessary. I think it makes sense to stand with Him beside me as my Ally; and that the others on that battlefield facing the devil be of God's choosing rather than mine.

CHURCH BODY

If my intent is to learn, consequently grow, possibly change, I need to be in a situation in which challenging discussion and questioning is acceptable; probably the reason I loved, and currently miss graduate-school classes. Why do we Christians seem to be so threatened by questions? Why do we not ask questions? Am I the only one who stumbles to define Christian terms such as sin, redemption, absolution, meekness, essentials, faith, and yet sense discomfort when I ask for definitions within the Christian community? I believe the fact that questions are not asked is not to be taken as an indication that people do not <u>have </u>questions. It has not been uncommon in my experience for people to come up to me after a class and whisper: "I am so glad you asked that question; I had the same question." In grad school, I attributed it to the younger ages; however, in the church setting, the people whispering their thanks were generally not younger than I.

Why is it that some of us state that when we are struggling with certain 'hurts', we prefer to go to those outside the church community for support or help? Why did I for months and months, all the time praying for something that would help me be closer to the person I dreamed of becoming, refuse to open a book placed on my table containing valuable answers? ... Because it was written by a Christian author and because my church experience taught me that I am a sinner, consequently I am required to seek forgiveness and to forgive because I must be meek. My expectations were that a Christian author would address the concepts as surely as a church body would. Is it the individuals, or is it just accepted precepts, within a group that determine our joining a given group? Is there something about a church group or setting that sets it apart from other groups?

Any person who calls self 'Christian', surely wishes to be an upstanding Christian...one who is striving to be right with God and to maintain an example and ministry that would label him/her as such to anyone with whom he/she comes into contact. An upstanding Christian would certainly also be expected to follow church doctrine. This presents a tall order for any human. It also presents plenty of opportunities for observations, opinions, and judgment, or growth.

If one's personal goals are in alignment with perceived church doctrine, however deemed to be unobtainable at the present time, he/she may feel required to live a facade when with individuals in the church body. I, for one, have experienced the difficulty in trying to keep up the facade while emotionally broken and, at the same time, trying to protect the outside visible-emotional wholeness. Would a requirement of an upstanding Christian be one who maintains emotional wholeness? Is that a goal of the picture your church body tries to present to the outside world (thereby to be followed by church body)? When I am in a place of emotional brokenness, might I choose to seek support and/or help outside the church body? There have been times when I, and some of my Christian friends, have chosen to not turn to a church family for support. Would this present a question possibly required by a church body to address?

Statistics state that one in three have been abused. Are you of the opinion the statistics cannot possibly pertain to your church body? Is it possible that, if I choose to take a walk through the woods in preference to attending your church service, I return home with less stress than had I been in attendance in your church setting?

If I have chosen to attend a church service even though I am aware of feeling threatened, I will likely be seated with my back covered. Please let me know if you are approaching me. I will probably be sitting on the end of the pew; please do <u>not</u> block my way out of the pew when talking to me. Do not stand over me by putting one hand on the pew at my back and the other hand on the pew in front of me (a common stance, in my experience). And, at the end of the church service, <u>please</u> do not block the exit doors by greeting and meeting, preventing me from a comfortable exit of my choosing. We all are capable of triggering another's thoughts by our words or actions, oftentimes without our knowledge. Perhaps it would be wise when in a church setting, or any place, to keep in mind that we all have a life story unique to us; consequently, there is no other exactly like yours or mine.

Sometimes, people recognize the need for tangible/or concrete... the sense of a touch or the sound of a voice... or another with whom to have a conversation when struggling without being judged. I have been told this concept defines a job of the church family. (My definition of 'church body' is the group of people regularly attending a particular church.) If this is true, why am I encountering so many other Christians who, like I, are consciously choosing to <u>not</u> be an active attendee in a church? I believe many, if not all, of us in this situation are aware of a hollowness deep within because of our choice; and yet we continue to stay on the same chosen path. For me, personally, the question loomed: "Is it possible for me to be climbing the healing ladder while honestly participating within a church body?"

Does not God know me better than I know myself? If this concept is a truism, then does not the question of why would one consider projecting a facade within the church environment require examination? Is the issue hypocrisy (a word I hear often)? Or, perhaps, could it be church doctrine? (I believe Christians in my environment desire to follow Christian teachings not dependent on them being active participants in a particular church body.) Could the issue be the manner with which we, as Christians, present ourselves? When approached by someone hurting and questioning; could I possibly, while talking with them, give the impression I am 'talking down to them', 'preaching at them' or, perhaps 'judging them'? My guess is that the depth or intensity of personal aspects in one's healing is somewhat dependent on the level of support, enabling or, perhaps condemnation of significant others. If one is in a church family, is it possible he/she is present because he/she views Christians as significant others?

How important is it for us to clearly define our assigned, or better yet, claimed role in our lives as Christians living on this earth? If one accepts the concept that we are all sinners; then, what concept is it that places a Christian on a higher pedestal than anyone else, while we are all struggling to make the choices we determine as necessary for this present day?

Is it possible that we Christians have, perhaps unconsciously, accepted an assumption that, because we have a certain 'label' attached to who we are; we have assumed the 'right' to treat our fellow humans not having the same label as somehow beneath us? Is it also possible that we may unconsciously assume the same 'right' in our association with fellow Christians resulting in a fellow Christian choosing to live a facade when in our presence? Is the manner with which I secretly identify myself as Christian, in relation to all other humans within my environment, a determining factor in my treatment of all others?

I was asked by a friend the other day to define the word, Christian. I am thankful the question was asked because it caused me to ask myself some serious questions. I do not know about you, but I have identified myself as Christian most of my life without carefully defining the term to myself. Within my professional life, had I been consistently using terminology in presentations I could not define; I am certain uncomfortable consequences would have resulted. If, in fact, my fundamental Christian beliefs are as important to me as I believe them to be, then why do I not define Christian concepts as easily as I did the professional concepts? Why do I use Christian terminology expecting others to understand my meaning? I do not have a theological background. It is entirely possible, therefore, that my definition of many terms may not agree with another's definition. Do I have a responsibility to God, others within my environment, and myself that I have not claimed?

Is it possible that one's life story may impact the definition he/she assigns terminologies like forgiveness, sin, and absolution for instance? Is it possible that one's life story may impact the struggle one has in aligning one's life to the Christian ethics being presented in conversations by church membership; or, perhaps even in his/her own life-time accepted definition of certain terms?

Dear Church Leadership:

Today is a going-to-church day for many of my friends; some of whom are questioning if they will continue attending; some are not attending, and some who are attending comment regarding the fact I question so much so often. I have been surprised, however, at the number of people I have met who are in the same position as I, by choosing not to be in attendance in a church service today.

Initially I was surprised at the number of fellow Christians among my friends who are or have been in this struggle. I think it would probably be safe to state that one thing we share is a type of sense, important to our personal well-being within us, that is missing when we are not actively participating within a 'church body' and yet, we choose to remain outside. Perhaps another commonality is that they feel like I…not yet strong enough…if a facade is required, the church is not a safe place for me.

By the way, please do not allow yourself to be naive enough to not be open to the fact that sexual inappropriateness may possibly be an issue within your church in some way. Please do not believe that, because you have not been made aware of the possibility, it does not, therefore, exist. In the car one evening on our way to a stage production, a friend and I discovered we were both 'victims' of the same church official.

The thought occurred to me that, perhaps I could explain the conflict to you that another may be experiencing. I am trying to define a concept in your life that you would struggle to explain, and I do not know how...driving, maybe? I remember when I was teaching another to parallel park. I did not know I could not explain to him what to do until he was stopped beside the other car and looked at me ready with the car in reverse and asked which way to turn the wheel. I could not tell him. Try to identify something in your life that would put you in the same position as I while sitting in the car... something that is so much a part of you, it is as if it has moved into your unconsciousness; it is so ingrained within you, it is something you do without thought. It is something that you cannot explain to another...got it?

* * *

Perhaps, if you are now in this place, you can possibly try to step into this picture, as bizarre as it seems. Try to picture yourself at about third to fifth grade:

Picture the person in your early life who was responsible for your care coming to your bed and waking you by hurting you in some way some nights. You do not know which nights it will happen. He/she smells that awful way and acts that strange, scary way...it hurts... but you must be quiet and are afraid to go to the bathroom when it is over. If you just disappear maybe you'll be safe; so, you just pull up the covers and hide like always. You can hide now because it is done...until next time.

Now it is the next day and you are outside 'playing'...give yourself a minute to try to identify with what you are <u>really</u> doing. You are probably glad you do not have to go to school as you are very tired. School is a lot like home...hard.

When you are called to go into the house, how do you react secretly? You are told to go to the store to get an item; you do not recognize the item, but you do know if you ask, you will be in trouble (the person sending you is the other adult responsible for your care). These people take you to church so you pray on the way to the store that someone will give you the right thing so you will be able to escape the consequences of arriving at home with the wrong thing. At the store, they knew what to give you so, if you are lucky, you will get to go right back outside again when you get home.

It is years later, home and school are still not easy, you have not been allowed to participate in some fun activities at school (the maypole outside on the lawn, for one) because they were/are against your religion. I am not certain if you are just getting out of grade school. I think, maybe, you are in sixth to eighth grade; but you have just performed in a play at church. The church people have probably been telling you how good you are, but you want to hear that from the ones in the front seat of the car; they are leaders in the church too, but they have not acknowledged you. They are the two adults in the prior paragraphs. You are now big and sitting in the back seat with your sibling. The car has not started yet, so you ask them how you did in the play. You keep looking in the rear-view mirror for the recognition from the front seat of the car...the eyes look right back deeply into you and the voice states: "No better than anyone else." The car starts and you are being taken back to your home to live the life it offers you for the day.

Years have passed since you began your healing process and numerous changes have taken place as you ascended the ladder's steps. Whenever possible; although you identified yourself as Christian, you consciously avoided anything...other than attendance at a performance by a family member...pertaining to a church activity. It was also at that time that you began going to birth-family members and friends with questions openly trying to seek out information for help in identifying various puzzle pieces pertaining to scenarios you were recalling from your life-story pages, consequently forcing your birth family into a position they did not want to be experiencing.

More years have passed since you initially took that action with few sporadic family gatherings compared to other families within your environment. Currently, only one of your past caretakers is still living and you are fulfilling a request to visit. Others in your life see you as successful. You immediately began working at various jobs out of high school not seeing college in your future. Then, you married and could save money to better yourself by going to college and successfully gain higher degrees. You are now a professional person, receiving accolades within your profession, very uncommon within your birth family. Most assume you are definitely 'living the good life'.

Your past caretaker is no longer a church leader but still an attendee, and you spent this morning attending her church with her. Currently she is busy ridiculing and belittling you and your current profession while she is washing the dinner dishes as you sit at the kitchen table drinking your coffee. You are consciously struggling to make your emotions and behavior align with your self-definition as a Christian, as you try to reflect the pain.

*   *   *

Thank you for trying to put yourself in this person's life for the above few paragraphs. An individual I know well has lived the above scenarios and could very easily be in your church body; or maybe it is the sibling, the one who also was a child in that household. The individual described in the above paragraphs desired to be an upstanding Christian his/her whole life and still does. This person still identifies him/herself as a Christian and is striving to follow church teachings. You may each consider the other a friend. He/she may have equal number of degrees as you; however, with a different emphasis. Your educational background includes theology, his/hers does not. You need advice within his/her field, you go to your friend. He/she does the same.

How are you presenting the important concepts of Christian teachings to this individual? Concepts such as forgiveness and meekness, and sin? Is it possible important concepts are presented as 'rules' with no definitions?

Please, as church leadership, recognize that each person within your classes is going to relate to what you present from his/her own life-story personal experience. Now, please put yourself in the place of a member of a class and not the presenter: Someone broke into your home…going through your drawers…stole things important to you; today you are sitting in a church building attending a class, or a sermon, and the presenter is using a break-in as an example within the context of the presentation. Where is your mind going to go; the same place as your friend sitting next to you who has never had a like experience? I do not think so. What about a sexual-abuse survivor? Do not our bodies automatically react to certain stimuli? When one touches a hot burner, will not the hand jerk back?

I have permission to use the following scenario by calling the boat operator, Tam: A co-worker, familiar with Tam's life story, called asking Tam to go across the bay to help a friend of hers struggling with sexual abuse. Tam immediately jumped in the boat to go find the woman and take her for a boat ride and private chat. While riding in the boat, Tam explains that she felt an urging to say something like this to the stranger with her: "I have begun to recognize that I am healing because there are now times when I think about my abuse that I do <u>not</u> also have the repugnant sexual sensation which always accompanied any recollections." Tam was surprised at the immediate and forceful response from her rider whose mouth and eyes opened wide as in shock, as she leaned across the boat towards Tam and shouted a question like: "Are you saying the day will come when I no longer have to live with that?" I believe this is a common, hated, secretive experience that many if not all sexually abused people suffer when triggered and will never voice it to another human being. Please remember this when helping another.

I also personally believe that, if one has been abused, he/she has been taught a self-definition likened to an object rather than a human. Consequently, if a believer, may also be dealing with issues accepted as fundamental within Christian doctrine, and struggling to align same with a sense of decency and self-worth when opening the door to attend a church service. And please do not allow yourself to be naive enough to not be open to the possibility that a sexual abuser is a member, or perhaps an officer, or a greeter of your church body.

Your audience has a variety of life experiences about which you know nothing, and I believe some about which you will never know. But, in my opinion, I do not stand alone in having lived a life that presents triggers to me that I cannot control which will be experienced by something you, at some point, will state either in a presentation or in a conversation.

Please define your terms. If concepts such as humility, meekness, forgiveness are included in the presentations or conversations which I expect within a Christian setting; however, probably never within a non-Christian setting, what conclusions will be drawn from the verbiage you use. You may know what you mean by it; but step out of 'you' and into the mind of another and read your text. Perhaps the chances are great that the survivor will not ask the questions your presentation may have brought to his/her mind. This person who has been taught by significant others, or his/her own body, that he/she is 'not as good as' may be sitting in front of you with the same desire you have to be a responsible Christian. How are your words speaking to this individual? If the person chooses to not ask you questions, these words may be the only determining factor as to the individual's returning to another church service.

Is climbing the healing ladder while, at the same time living according to church doctrine, possible within the environment of your church body; or are the two concepts in opposition? If an individual is at the place in which a life situation has forced him/her into a position of slipping off the path leading to the attainment of achieving God's purpose for his/her life; is your presentation of church doctrine deterring the return to that path for the individual? Is it possible that your presentation may be interpreted to be saying that it is sinful to respectfully protect self? If one defines self as Christian; is it possible for an attendee to be placed in a position that to continue in the church body, he/she cannot remain in alignment with his/her desired definition of self? Does each individual professing like beliefs have like responsibilities within the belief's structure? Do the same principles apply to all equally?

What about the member sitting next to this individual? The one who has lived the opposite life? Oh, of course, he/she has lived such experiences as: loved ones have died, sickness has caused missed work and school days and various unexpected expenses, the kids need to be called at times to drive to doctor appointments; and then, there's the grandchildren's birthdays and sports to keep the calendar full. But robberies, abuse...that awful stuff that happens to people he/she does not know, in his/her opinion; this person is considering following the pattern of friends and stopping all television in the house because the exposure to such 'going-ons' is too unpleasant!

Such describes some of the most wonderful, caring, down-to-earth, pleasant people I have ever met. To put them in a situation I have just put you in in the preceding activity, without his/her permission would be cruel, in my opinion.

So, I also hold the opinion that I am glad I am not in your shoes, as both are possibly sitting side by side as you walk up to the podium to present the lesson you have prepared for this hour.

Do you not have the responsibility to treat each of these members with the same consideration? Do not these two people have like responsibilities to each other as well as to the rest of the membership? Do they not have the right to anticipate respect from any other in the church environment? Do they not also have equal rights and responsibilities to themselves: to heal their hurts, to seek until they find the answers to their questions? (I now realize that I, personally, for years had not claimed my responsibility to seek to find answers to my many questions regarding the Bible and church. I labeled such a responsibility as one the church was to claim and present to me. The Bible was too complicated for me to comprehend.)

The church leader, most instrumental in my current personal Bible study, continually encouraged the congregation by suggesting various aids. Consequently, I was introduced to Bible Commentaries and Dictionaries currently on my personal bookshelves and he defined terms within his sermons. These tools have enabled me to experience an excitement and enjoyment in studying the Bible beyond what I had experienced or would have expected. In addition, this church leader is the first individual in that position with whom I have scheduled appointments to discuss, in a church office, personal questions or concerns regarding Biblical concepts.

Following are some comments, issues, and suggestions I have along with some offered by others asking me to include regarding:

Church Safety

In my opinion, the definition of this topic depends on one's location on the healing ladder. The manner with which he/she reacts in a discussion of church doctrine or church safety, or in church classes or other lessons varies according to where one is on the ladder at a given time. For instance, when I say, 'love myself' with all that statement signifies for me; do you think 'new age' and judge? Is not pride one of the greatest of sins? Paramount at times in my healing, was to learn how to feel a love and respect for myself instead of the self-loathing that I, and I believe many others, experience. I struggled years on the healing ladder before I was able to accept that I am as deserving as you to 'suck the same air as you'. In openly discussing this aspect of my healing within the church community, I have struggled with being preached at and receiving pamphlets warning of the terrible dangers of 'new-age' thinking from Christian friends when I was <u>finally</u> healthy enough to not only attend church, but to become vocal.

When I am in the victim mentality; certain definitions may be of utmost importance to me such as humility, servitude, love one to another. I am placed in a precarious plight because I am a Christian, and I desire to have Christian support. When I am vulnerable, certain definitions may tend to confirm my self- beliefs of unworthiness, evil, and disgusting. When I am in victim mentality, I not only hold this opinion of myself; but I cannot feel His presence as He has cast me aside recognizing I am totally all my abusers labeled. Defining terms may be an unrecognizable help to anyone in the victim place in front of you. Although, when I am in the place of survivor rather than victim, defining of terms is also a huge help when offered in presentations or conversations... I wish it would be more common.

My belief is that in any church gathering, trauma victims/survivors will be present with their placement on the healing ladder varying, possibly dependent on your presentation. Their thinking process as they sit before you might be extremely literal, particularly if their life story involves beatings for not specifically following given instructions.

Physical Considerations:

If I put my arms out straight in front of me and turn in a circle, my personal space is defined for anyone else. No one in a church body should come closer to me than the circle circumference defines without my permission. If you are facing me and approaching me to talk and I step back, I am telling you that you have crossed the line into my comfortable personal space; do not continue coming at me...stop and tell me what you wish to say. This is a huge issue for sexual-abuse survivors; particularly those of us who have been inappropriately treated by church attendees/leadership. Always be aware of personal boundaries when approaching/touching/ hugging a person you do not know well. The possibility exists that one out of three people have had experiences discussed within these pages.

Have you ever thought about this? When you are giving a sermon, or teaching while standing, you are no doubt above me while talking; thus, forcing me to look up to you. Any time this is the case, we are physically not on equal ground. Consequently, assuming I have gathered the required nerve to come to your church office for a conference, what will it look like to me? When I am in your office, is there a big barrier between you and me, such as a desk? Do we have level eye contact, or are you looking down at me? Are you near something you may tend to glance at periodically, such as a phone/computer? Perhaps you could sit in my chair before my arrival and note any barriers.

You may act in a manner threatening to another. <u>However, do not automatically assume you have acted in a threatening manner for a survivor to be threatened.</u> He/she might be threatened by the fact the building is a church. (I am on a Sunday morning currently knowing a big number of people are present and in close quarters; but for me personally, the biggest threat is the entrance covered by the 'greeters who I do not know and yet am required to approach and allow them to probably touch me, maybe even running out to me with an umbrella in the rain to walk with me.) He/she may be triggered to the extent that your simply being involved with church may cause one to identify you as an enemy or, at minimum, a possible threat if, for no other reason, you may use 'terror words' such as sin, confront, forgive, forget. In my opinion, one's silent reaction, or visible reaction, may vary from one meeting to the next … depending upon his/her location on the healing ladder. I can guarantee you that it is the case for me, so far always if I have been absent for an extended period and not on the healing ladder in the interim. I do not blame the church family for this issue recognizing they are trying to be happy people who wanting me to know they are so excited for me to be coming today and want me to come back…I try not to define it as threatening and false recognizing it could be spiritual warfare. One tool I use is to be carrying things that require me to not be able to touch another…it seems to help others to not want to touch me; if you have this issue, try it… I carry water and a Bible with pen, notebook, etc.

We are all capable of triggering another's thoughts by our words or actions, often totally without our knowledge. Perhaps the strongest requests I can make of you is to always assume the victim will be in your audience and to try to describe your thoughts accordingly, defining any pertinent concept. I am familiar with pastors who are practicing this and others within the church body have asked me if I have noted a positive change in their sermons. And always be respectful of the personal physical space of those in the congregation (including the 'greeters'). It may be that choices you make regarding these two concepts will determine the safety factor of your church body to an individual climbing the healing ladder.

SUPPLEMENT to CHURCH BODY

1. Please take the time to consider and discuss any pertinent information you identified within this section.

2. Please know that there will be those within your body who will be praising you; however, you may not be able to hear the voices.

CHURCH-BODY ADDENDUM

To those within the church family who desire to help others dealing with abusive situations: Picture with me, please, that we are sitting in a church-family meeting and the assignment is to give a definition of an abusive situation. Scenarios have included a child being beaten (hit and kicked), sexual abuse, and an adult saying something to a child that had hurt the feelings of the child. Obviously, one thing to keep in mind always is that we may, quite easily, define important words in our conversations differently. And our life stories are not written identically, even if we are in the same family.

I believe you are taking on a difficult task, as my experience is that it is hard to understand, if not impossible, someone who has experienced a life-story extremely different than yours. I am uncomfortable with seatbelts, increased when in another's car. But have ridden with friends who do not preach to me about the importance of wearing a seatbelt accepting me as an equal, even recognizing my escalation and coming around the car to <u>silently</u> unhook it from me quickly when I am struggling to get 'untied'. Because he/she would 'get it'...perhaps not agree with it, perhaps not identify with it--but, 'get it'. And I know that I cannot identify with someone complaining about family members who bring flowers for their yard, but do not stay hours planting them. I have found it is helpful to have certain uncomfortable situations labeled allowing avoidance and me to experience a pleasant relaxing day today by choosing to keep the past life-story book closed and on the shelf. I can choose to not continue a negative conversation with another today. I can choose to not turn to the ones who lecture me regarding the seatbelt when I am struggling with a trigger. And I can possibly choose to quickly deal with the trigger, close the book, put it on the shelf, turn and step back into the positive today offers without involving anyone else. I cannot change my past and refuse to negate the life that defines me. But the God I worship has given me the free-will gift allowing me choices as to how I might live on this day.

Abuse is an uncomfortable topic for people listening as well as for those sharing. It is not an unusual experience for me to be with another who has just shared an abuse scenario with me (especially if we do not 'know one another') and to be horrified and apologetic that he/she had done it. Such happenstances verify a sense of 'trepidation'. Although I totally 'get it', I have made a personal choice to no longer live a facade to feel accepted or equal with others. This recent decision has provided me with a problem I do not recall discussing with another in the church family. So, I will ask you to keep it in mind while reading this addendum as will in typing it. I recognize that my life story is not conducive to a warm, fuzzy environment in which to chat comfortably; and, like all others, I have a responsibility to treat others with respect I desire from them. My definition of my problem is this: My past scenarios are oftentimes abusive; and, unfortunately, are often the ones triggered while with others. Consequently, I ask you to consider the question I ask myself: Are there 'rules' that are required within this church body that prevent me from quickly sharing the puzzle piece or to answer a question without considering possible responses from church-body members? I expect any believer would prefer to turn to the church family for understanding and support; however, I am familiar with situations in which this is not an option taken. If I ask why, the answer invariably refers to judging and/or preaching. My personal experience feeling 'judged' or 'preached at' include:

(A) Being told in the church that I was not asked to be one to pray because I do not believe in God. I had made the statement that the trouble with God is that He is not concrete. (I am thankful today that God is more concrete to me than ever before in my life as I am consciously aware of His presence daily. He also has shown me in concrete ways that he knows exactly what my current needs are.) I find it interesting, however, not one in the church family ever asked me what I meant by that statement and it never occurred to me that another adult would not understand what I was saying...we live different lives. Or, perhaps, others who have struggled like I and been in a place in which they feel broken to the point in which they could not feel God's presence simply choose not to allow others to have that personal information. Hopefully, they did not hear the conversation in which I was told that I was not a believer.

(B) Feeling comfortable enough in a church meeting to share why I disagreed with another's identification of a text, I automatically and openly referenced a scenario in my life-story triggered by their comment. But, instead of that conversation continuing, I was immediately told: "Well, you know, you need to forgive". I was disappointed and felt judged. Why? Because my experience in conversations is that people commonly reference a personal-life experience to make a point and I had become comfortable enough in the class that I did not ponder the possible consequences of what I was going to say prior to saying it. The response to my statement erased the level of comfort for me in the class. By that time, I was at a good place with the forgiveness issue in the scenario I shared; consequently, it no longer had the negative control of me it once did. But obviously is, and always will be a part of who I am; just as your experiences identify you. However, nobody in the class bothered asking me <u>my</u> opinion, but rather identified what I needed to do in their opinions. In earlier years, I would have walked out and never gone back to the church. But, in that meeting that day I identified myself as an equal to others in the room. God had already helped me to believe that these people are good, caring people who have not experienced like situations and cannot identify with me anymore than I can identify with many of their shared experiences. Also, I was stronger that day than the day in which the scenario took place in my life. I was able to be strong enough to lean on God's gift of an equal to others and, rather than leaving, I chose to ask a question. I asked very loudly to all, exactly what that would look like in the situation I just described and to provide me with the exact steps I 'need' to take. In my opinion, I did not get either answered clearly and no definition of forgive. I do not remember saying more and the class continued.

The personal results from that class that jumped out at me for those of us who desire to help the ones struggling are: 1. Do not use terms that I cannot define. 2. Do not give directions that I cannot define. 3. Should the ability to use a personal example experienced in one's life to be shared openly in a class be based on how 'comfortable' the story is to others?....... I made the statement in the class because I felt it was appropriate and that others with like stories would believe the same. The other important thing, in my opinion, regarding that meeting is that after that class, a lady I did not know (and do not recall seeing since) came up to me very quietly and thanked me for what I had said and shared her 'like' abuse story with me standing off to the side of the group .... which happens various times when I share something in my abuse experience. Sometimes, it is simply a thankyou; but always it is done very quietly and after the close of the gathering. I never assume that I am the only one in the room with a like story; but I do assume I am the only one who is going to claim such; which remains a frustration to me within a church family. But that day, I did not think before speaking and was surprised, and would still like to discuss the comments regarding the passage. My desire always, when I feel the need to get clarifications or ask for help, is to turn to another believer with whom I feel 'safe' and when I desire 'concrete'; I think any believer feels the same.

Vocabulary can be important in conversations. Not only definitions of words used, but the word alone may be threatening. Some of the most used words can be a threat to a 'victim' and still are at times for me in conversations... 'need to/have to/should'. They are all telling me I am not satisfactory nor acceptable in the speaker's opinion and there is something for which I am responsible that has not been accomplished. Consequently, I battle feeling judged...without a concrete jury. It was thirty years ago that I was wallowing around in the pit trying to stand; and began seeking clarification as to why. I was refusing to turn to God and struggling with self-concept as I was only looking to other humans to verify my equality. I had already spent years avoiding church services as much as possible and another thirteen years of studying and counseling before turning back to the church as a regular attendee. (I guess that provides a good definition of our Heavenly Father, doesn't it? He has convinced me that He has tons of patience.) I avoided turning to anything 'religious' to help my healing process because I knew I was a sinner (then, now, and for as long as I remain on this earth) and that I was required to forgive because I knew I was a believer. But a requirement for me to deal with forgiveness and the sin issue was that I had to heal to the point that I could feel equal to others. I was able to 'get out of me' in my past life-story scenarios and study individuals in the puzzle piece trying to not use my personal bias. And I had done all that work prior to the referenced class-experience.

However, the class experience is also an example of another helpful description of a possible unidentified issue within any conversation regarding an abusive situation. I have identified that, when I am in conversations in which I feel I am being judged, I react by defending self; consequently, I am not 'looking beyond me'; but rather, remaining in the negativity of the current situation. I assume any abused person has the same issue. I find situations which force me to stay within the scenario when I am asking for help to close that book, are situations I prefer not to repeat. When I was attending that class, I had been a survivor for years. In earlier years, the impact on me would have been different in many ways. I can tell you that my definition of a particular 'church family' is defined by experiences in various meetings and personal conversations with individual members of the group. The sermons determine what I will be able to learn to help my personal Biblical studying. The availability of taped sermons is also a valuable tool I use.

Some of what I will be saying may come from college-class experience. However, it is my thinking that my life story has a greater impact on my beliefs and thoughts today than does my formal education. I can guarantee you one thing: The person you wish to help will have triggers in his/her life just as you do; however, expect the definitions to vary. I believe it is also wise to assume that you will never hear all that pertains to the situation being described. But He/she may be impacted for years with the results of your discussions. I realize I have and still am benefiting from same. I think believers must have the ability to stand on the battlefield to fight the life on earth brings. Therefore, gaining that ability is paramount and while climbing a ladder it is impossible to stand, let alone wear armor! It may require some time to identify and claim personal responsibility along with a healthy self-identification to feel the strength available to walk on the path He has laid for one. For me, the time required lessened as my height on the ladder-climb increased. And, on the Foundation and in the Light, it may only take minutes to turn a negative into positive in this day. Also providing another reason why I choose to stay in the present tense when asking for help. I assume the same applies to another I am trying to help as the only negativity regarding the abusive scenario that may be changed, is what is happening today.

Another issue which may be in a current life story is a lack of memories. I assume you would agree that a 'memory' means you can picture the whole scenario in your mind. I have more snippets here and there than I have complete scenarios. I now assume that upon high-school graduation, walking into the adult life I wanted, putting on the facade, and leaving others behind; I mentally dug a hole and shoved my past life into it. I have read that stuffing experiences causes one to bury the good with the bad creating a void which has at times, not only been frustrating for me but also embarrassing. But I have also read, and agree, that God does not change the past scenario when returning it to the individual, which can be a problem in a conversation in which another is asking for help as the descriptions could be confusing. Consequently, this person now asking for your help, is not the person you identified on that nice walk you shared last week, but rather is a 'victim' sharing a hurtful, and probably terribly embarrassing situation that is only being shared because the individual is tired of the control it has today and has decided you can be trusted to not share it. But, if the helper asks questions <u>regarding the scenario</u>, the 'victim' is being forced to stay within the scenario re-experiencing the pain. Which is why I prefer to keep my part of a conversation, as a helper, in the present tense. We cannot change the past; but perhaps we can change the power the past has over the individual today. So, I prefer to ask questions like, perhaps: Have you defined the affect that has on you today .... What do you need to change to make tomorrow a better day for you to experience? .... How would you define the goal for that change to be accomplished? .... Do you feel ready to identify the steps you could start taking today? My <u>thinking</u>, as a helper as well as when asking for help, is that God has allowed the trigger; so, the purpose is to define what needs to be done today to follow His desired path.

My personal experience has taught me an interesting concept that I identify today: God does not force me to have memories in answering many of my questions. I believe God has, in the past and is today, only giving me information required to follow what He is asking me to do in this day; therefore, allowing me much more positive than negative! I have been able to identify answers he has gifted me by using the concreteness I require through people and situations currently in my life. It no longer surprises me to gain insight from a conversation that triggers an unanswered question but also leads to verifications for me. Proving to me that my Heavenly Father was always with me and is also aware of my current needs; and then seems to meet the need I have in the terms of my learning style! It is interesting how the insights that come help me; but can also help others. I believe He has all my scenarios at His disposal and often uses today to provide insights I need to follow His desired path. The lessons I learned in the class I described is an example of God showing me concretely in turning a past negative scenario into a positive. It is also an example of how a past painful experience no longer triggers negativity in me. As in that class, I identified it as an example from my life to make my point in the question I was asking...nothing more. My reaction of some class members to my comment tells me, personally, how powerful the God I worship is as the effects of that life-story page had pained me for years. But, in describing it in class that day, I used it as nothing but an example of my line of thinking. And, fellow past-victim, if you are one reading this, please remember that same God is waiting to do the same for you! Your choice! It is a gift and fascinating to recognize how He works! My response in class that day was as natural as taking a sip of the water sitting in front of me. So much so that the response of the class took me a few seconds to define what was happening and why! So, what is the question to be asked? How is the definition of this class situation to be made?

I seldom am negatively triggered today, but also have the ladder techniques in my pocket as the process can be used quite quickly with practice...sometimes in minutes. Often in my case, clarity was found by studying puzzle pieces in which significant others are saying things...sometimes hurtful to me. However, God allows me to hear the same thing differently with the removal of revenge and anger with which I heard from others when choosing to <u>not</u> work with Him. His directions allow 2+2=4, which enables me to take a very deep breath and a big step forward today. Consequently, a past issue triggered by common daily questions from others honestly may be defined as a gift from Him; sometimes even allowing me to consider it a positive polished to help another. We each have individual memories which help form the person we are in this day. They are different; and we are not identical to one another, allowing us to learn from each other if we choose to look beyond ourselves to do so. Sometimes, however, I do not know about you, but it's hard for me to practice that thinking with proper respect. So, I am still tweaking goals!

An unexpected trigger recently took control of me that may clarify for you how powerful memories can be and how quickly they can control a past- abuse victim. But, also, with practice, how quickly the trigger can be controlled...this scenario happened within

2-3 minutes; but was one I prefer not to be repeated. It is possible that you have had a like experience in your life, but with a completely different reaction. <u>When one is sharing with you their abuse, it may take them back to that place...be careful.</u> I was lying on the bed of a ' pet scan' a week ago today and the gal said that it would help the test if she taped my arms. So, I took a deep breath and said 'ok'; then she crossed my arms and started to put tape around them. I kept trying to convince myself that I was strong enough to 'take it'. I think within the time she had gone around twice before cutting the tape, I was experiencing the trigger. Most of me was in that trigger and not in the present...I was that child tied up in that closet that quickly. I yelled at her to take it off...now! And within my head I was screaming PLEASE respect me, do not preach, judge, or again tell me the "right way" to view this scenario you are providing me in my life's page right now (which she had done prior to putting the tape on). If she had not turned to take it off when I yelled at her to do so and continued walking across the room to lay the roll of masking tape on the counter........ I am glad I do not know how that day a week ago would have turned out. I was back in that space in the past; however back into the present by the time she threw the tape into the can by the counter across the room; probably about 9' away from me lying on the machine. I may be the only who has ever shared a story like this to you; but I do not stand alone with like triggers. Although I, obviously, recognized the request as a trigger; I never expected it to take that kind of control. I honestly felt I could manage it by closing my eyes and breathing deeply for the required time. But I am also amazed as to how fast I was pulled back into present tense after having gone back so far (God thing!). Believe me, I <u>now have a renewed respect for the others with whom I am trying to help having the courage to share their stories and will be repeating to you and praying that I will never 'not take the tape off' the one telling me the story asap and always remember to not force him/her to stay in that abusive situation for one more second of time!</u>

I want to always accept the possibility that in conversations I have with others about their abuse, they are re-experiencing the scenarios they are describing in the conversation which could be worthlessness--- the self-identification of not being a living, breathing, capable individual with rights given to same, fear, physical sensations, pain. So, please .... I beg you, as well as myself, that we walk carefully, monitoring ourselves as much or more as the person with whom we are speaking in these conversations.

Standing in the LIGHT allows me to be ok with a lingering question instead of an answer. I can now readily accept that I am not GOD. Therefore, perhaps it does not hold the importance I think it does, right? I realized, as I climbed higher on the ladder, less answers were required because I began to understand that the past story does not change with more clarity; the only thing I can change is me in my present. Although I believe it is important to honestly study self to get well acquainted initially, and to define emotions clearly, and claim them allowing one to 'get the right pill for the problem'. (It's my understanding from many doctors that early diagnosis can be important and sometimes the negative is required to be identified to experience the positive.) However, why not allow the person who experienced the trigger the responsibility to identify the negativity it causes today and to determine the fastest and most practical manner with which it be controlled today? That is the individual who will live with the consequences.

So, could all of this be telling you and me that we are not the ones to determine where another is in his/her healing process? I have only lived my life story. I have not lived a relative's story, nor yours, nor the person sitting across from me sharing his/her story and his/her beliefs. I think it is not my place to define his/her conclusions, nor beliefs, nor life-story. Now that I believe I am equal to others, it is extremely important to me, personally, that others with whom I am speaking treat me as an equal and do not 'preach' to me about what is mandatory for me to do in my life today with no information as to how I define where I am today in my life. I define myself as a believer. Any memory I have of myself includes a belief that I am a sinner; I was raised in an environment that very carefully and consistently taught me that. And any memory I have of grade-school days through present includes a rule that I am required to forgive others because God's Word (the Bible) says to do so. I thank that pastor regularly who gave the definition of "I give up my right to hurt you for hurting me" for the word 'forgive' in a sermon. Put that with the Bible verse in which God states He will handle the revenge, and then put that with God seeing me as not beneath anyone else... Wow! That really helps me to stand in His armor with Him by my side and quote the Bible to Satan!

If the persons we are trying to help are believers, they know these things also. I 'm guessing these issues are as huge (and possibly as threatening) to them in their healing process as it is and has been throughout the entire healing process for me. If they indicate the latter is not so in any manner, I am going to be cautious because my goal is to help them gain the ability to label their choices today as positive. Maybe our job is not done. There may be something blocking the person's ability to follow a rule he/she identifies. As a helper, I do not want to put myself into the position of forcing another to be trying to break through a cement wall. I would prefer to perhaps help identify the wall that is preventing the use of the available strength God has provided His believers. Perhaps there are undefined issues preventing the ability to make choices positive for the individual. It took me years to have the strength to turn from others (concrete humanity) and turn to God enabling me to do that! However, my personal experience with other victims sharing is that they will introduce such issues with questions to me rather than I having to worry about when to discuss it. I feel they lived their stories, not I. I do not want the responsibility to define choices for another's life. I also always assume there is more to any story they have shared that I have not been told. If or when they bring it up, I assume they feel safe in the environment and have the trust in me not to judge. My prayer is that I will not judge, but rather realize God needs to control this conversation. I feel required to pray in this form because I readily accept that I probably have failed in the helper role more than the times I questioned the possibility.

I am thankful because my life story allows me credibility to help and learn from others who define self as victims. But abuse is uncomfortable for anyone to discuss. I believe helping another requires a desire to gain understanding of how to experience positivity today rather than to judge negativity. I also assume that anyone with a history of damaging abuse who has responsibilities in adult lives, particularly to others, probably have experienced living a facade to continue fulfilling requirements expected of them. My guess is that in our lives today, there may be numerous situations in which an individual is in a position feeling required to live a facade to enable them to converse with another. Although I recognize there are numerous times in which I am in a situation in which it may be disrespectful to mention a past negativity; I have a desire that within a church family, it would always be safe to do so in a conversation in which I am seeking help, guidance, or another's opinion in a struggle I am experiencing.

I am aware at times yet, being uncomfortable in a situation in which it is tempting to put that facade back on to simply participate in conversations. I do not believe this only happens within the church family. I was an adult attending college classes when others would come quietly to me after a class thanking me for a question. But I want to identify a church family as being different from others. Why shouldn't the church family provide all the opportunity to be who they honestly are and to be treated comfortably? At times it is difficult for me to comfortably associate with others and not feel uncomfortable with questions like: How are you? Do you have any concerns? What did you do today? Where have you been? Why weren't you there or here? Do you have a prayer request? Oh, you say you are studying...what are you studying? With whom did you spend Easter, Christmas, your birthday? Any one of these questions could cause others to put on a false front, or leave, or to not be present in the first place. Such questions sometimes cause me to be uncomfortable, or at least monitor how I am going to answer in church meetings; I wish it were not so.

When I began attending church regularly again; I learned much that has remained helpful. One goal fulfilled in that time was reading the Bible through for the first time and learning how to study it. Because I was attending a church with my car parked out front by the grocery store, people connected me with a church. Prior to that period, I had been able to be of assistance to others of all ages because of my life-story...sometimes only because of a boss who was willing to help and support me. I was comfortable feeling I knew how to help and answer questions. That changed in the new isolated environment in which I lived. For the first time, I began getting the 'hard questions' ... like the ones I had not wanted to address in my story. And it was in that church environment when I believe I first experienced spiritual warfare big time. There were times in which I would go to the balcony of the church, which was never used, to sit alone in a Sunday service; cry and fight the desire to leave the building knowing if I did, Satan would win the battle and I would not return. I do not recall anyone in the church questioning that behavior (the Pastor could see me while giving the sermon and was familiar with my story). In fact, one friend who realized what I was doing told me she would come up and sit by the stairway making sure no one came up the stairs. Others knew my story and never judged. The church was the place where I had to be strong and fight. Not everyone in attendance was supportive; I also experienced judging. But I was learning from the Pastor as well as others God put in that environment. I was recognizing God's presence. I was gaining self respect. And, in addition, a new sense of equality with 'church people' I had never before experienced. It helped me to lean into the strength I was beginning to recognize and to not turn and run when feeling broken or judged. I now, generally, feel an equality to any other human to the point that I share my story; even with people in church of more than fifteen people regularly attending a Sunday service! And, then turn and step into today with the book closed and on the shelf. It is something I would have never believed when I first put my foot on the healing ladder---the negatives <u>can be</u> turned into positives that are polished. They have helped another say things such as: wow, ... ok ... thanks ... I think I can do this too. Giving me reason to smile as I shut the door and turn back into today and walk across the room thanking God for giving me the story to help others and allowing me to be aware of the results. Fellow victim, know that we are equal in God's eyes, so you can have the same experience as I. Polishing the positive is even better if it was a negative originally; and, better yet, if I realize that having the strength to use it has helped another one of us!

An important issue has been brought to my attention now that I am back in the area I escaped for isolation and peace. Past and current church attendees ask me not to quit what I am doing; but to continue sharing and asking for believers within the church body with differing stories to try and 'get it'. I think if one is a believer, he/she has a desire to be able to turn to other believers for support when broken or suffering. But some of us will not because we do not want to be judged or preached at. At one time, women within a church family I joined had, individually, shared with me their abuse stories and, without identifying anyone, I asked each to form a group to help each other. None agreed. But one conversation sticks with me today... She was crying and said she would never talk to others in the church family about it because "What would those people think of me if they knew my story". I identify her as one of the most popular, highly-thought-of women in the church. Also, frequently, two other women I had asked to meet were sitting side by side within Sunday-morning services in front of me, neither realizing the support available sitting right next to them, while telling me I was the only one they would talk to about 'that'. God often has used these memories to encourage me in writing these addendums. Wouldn't it be wonderful if each one of us would be brave enough to remove facades and be supportive of each other? Imagine the power, the strength, as well as the companionship within a church family where none of us ever feel we need to put on a facade to be at ease within the church family. I know sexual-abuse survivors who are tough...I would be thrilled to have them surrounding me on the battlefield facing Satan! I wonder how Satan would feel about that... picturing that kind of strength in my mind makes me laugh, as I picture Satan turning and getting out of town like crazy! When I was not in a church body, there was something missing; but I did not trust myself to keep the facade in place to be accepted. When you are broken, you already know you need help, having someone point that out to you with what you need to do, or to change, or to believe did not help me have the strength to stand; but, rather, just verified that I was defining myself correctly when I was broken. I believe I have lots of company who have experienced the same.

It is important for me to remember that 'understanding' another whose life-story is totally different than mine seems an impossible assignment. But the decision I have reached is: That is not the assignment God is giving me; but, rather by listening carefully to another share and grow, He is providing me an opportunity to do the same. I have been taught helpful lessons from others with life stories with which I can, in no way, relate. I am not sure I can identify a time when I have partaken in a deep conversation and not felt I gained from it. I assume, throughout my whole life, I have hurt many others unintentionally; probably others whom I am unaware. But I want to believe most who state desires to help others are good people with good intentions. I think it is possible that abuse is so uncomfortable to all and what it teaches the 'victim' is so restrictive and degrading that too often for various reasons, the results are not addressed nor even identified.

Again, the importance of a sense of equality to others plays a role. Perhaps, even a requirement to stand, wear the armor of God, and face Satan. If one's abuse was the result of a family member, an individual would possibly be more hesitant to discuss it openly if it still has a negative effect today, depending on current circumstances. It is a possibility that the abuse was reported to another at the time, and the rule became to keep it a secret or it was not believed. In what way is this not saying to the victim: "you are a non-entity"? I question that a human could be a sexual-abuse survivor and not have questions. I also believe, that to heal (if the 'victim's definition of healing includes gaining closure to unanswered questions), discussions with people who may have insight is a desire. If the 'victim' is dealing with a family scenario, the healing process could easily result in additional issues; particularly if the rules have not changed. The 'family' in the scenario is not required to be 'birth'... but, could easily be a work family, a church family, a neighborhood. If the 'victim' is still, today, dictated negatively by the abusive situation; he/she could also, within certain environments, experience frequent triggers. I wrote an assignment in college in which I defined 'Result of, Abuse' as defining the 'victim' a non-entity. I believe there are situations in which that definition may easily apply for years within the 'victim's' perspective of self; although, with some, possibly only while in given scenarios involving the 'same others' within today's page of life's story. But do not try to convince me that the choice to not deal with negativity resulting from past life-story pages is a wise choice. One of the most important significant persons in my life from the first day told me various times: "I don't want to think about bad things, I put that in God's hands." ... I was recently informed that individual tried to commit suicide various times.

It is not unusual for me to be required to experience negative consequences for being bullheaded and pushing myself too hard; choices verified often with doctor bills in the mail. Careful self-monitoring; therefore, is a smart option for me in many situations. When I am with another, as a helper, it is wise for me to lean into the possibility of the other paying the consequences of the shared time rather than I. And my prayer is that the other leaves the conversation with positivity rather than negativity. My life has taught me that God's ways are definitely not the same as mine; nor is His timing.

I also agree with the belief I read in a Biblical reference that stated I cannot 'save' another; but God can, and He knows the person in front of me probably better than the person knows self! The person with whom I am talking has choices and will certainly be the one to pay consequences for same. I am extremely thankful that it is not my responsibility to save another. God did not give that responsibility to me; but rather to help and provide a safe place in which questions can be asked. In the process of helping another deal with abuse these are important concepts for me to consider: If I am not the person sharing the abuse experience, then I probably do not have the ability to provide clarity correctly. I was not present; and if I were, I probably would not have reacted in the same manner as this individual...not because there is a wrong and a right view, but because I did not live his/her history. I did not have the exact relationship to others in the scenario we shared. Now, if we did not even share the scenario, then my argument is even more important, right? So, maybe I, as a helper, if asked, may be able to offer some good ideas for the one in front of me to take to the inner room to ponder and pray about; then we could have a deep discussion about any questions that come up he/she identifies to address.

Healing from a physical result of abuse would, I hope, include meetings with a physician experienced in the identified diagnosis made by honest explanations of the scenario in which the damage was done initially. However, my personal emotive healing is exasperated if a helper to whom I go for help when emotionally struggling requires me to stay within the scenario by asking for specifics. Others with abusive pasts have agreed with my conclusion. The past is unchangeable, already happened, scars are there...some still noted in present, some not. Present always offers choices. In the first place, it is now my opinion that my abuse-isolated does not matter, for me personally, because I am now off the healing ladder and living in the Light in the present in which I am the only person I can change. The negative results have been labeled and addressed, and the scenario is in the past and cannot be changed. I define self as capable of standing on the battlefield of spiritual warfare next to Him protected by the armor of God. Consequently, my choice is to only spend time in looking at a past page if in doing so someone aids in continuing to follow Him.

I feel God's presence providing strength today. I do not feel a need for sympathy; even when I am asking another for input, I am generally a survivor rather than victim. I may choose to share because somebody is required to provide explanations for those with no experience to gain insight to be able to help. It is also a tool I may use in a conversation in the present tense; most often in answering a specific question to me regarding my past experiences. But with the thought that past cannot be changed...just, hopefully, the present negativity resulting from the past. I guarantee you that I do not stand alone with a like story. But there is a reason why the others in the group within the church family with a story like mine tell me their story privately after the meeting instead of joining the conversation openly. (They would probably have added important information that I have not experienced.) The response given to me impacts that person as much or more than my comment. Any time I am in a group with four or more, I assume someone else in the group has a like story as statistics have stated. I pray any conversation within in a church-family meeting in which I choose to be involved is beneficial to all in the manner He directs.

I may think I know another well; and then realize, when they call or ring my doorbell to request a deep chat that the portions of the story in that book that have never-before been heard, are showing struggles and strengths that I never would have guessed. I believe that to be true much more than any of us realize. However, the one ringing the bell is the human who is experiencing the negativity, not I. As a helper, when I am in this position after answering the door; I try hard to just listen until I hear why the conversation is taking place.

Reasons to <u>not</u> define the 'healing' of another as a helper may include the following possibilities: If I am talking to you about my abuse when hurting, I may be doing it to verbalize by helping to 'get it out' instead of inside controlling everything...an example of a time when I have turned to another for concreteness. Somehow stating it even to the wall verbally tends to make me feel stronger; it helps to accept that I exist and am not burying my life. When hurting, I may be talking to a trusted one because I think they may have some insights for me...something I have not included in trying to deal with the problem. Or I may (if I trust the other to not share what I am saying) ask for prayer if I feel I may error in conclusions I need to define. (The people I ask to pray for me pray that I will recognize His guidance. As I would rather not have to pay consequences in my life <u>again</u> for not paying attention to God's directions!) Please remember, helping me, that you have not lived my life-story, nor will you pay the consequences for the choices I choose for this day or the rest of my life. Please allow me the freedom to pick and choose my options. HE is the one I wish to have control of my life...not me... nor you. I know, from years of experience, the latter choice does not end that well.

I also think there may be an experience that seems so 'weird' one hesitates to share it ...this might be an example. An issue you or the one to whom you are speaking may have is that a trigger has been experienced of an abuse that had not been recalled before. (I call these the missing pieces in my big puzzle.) Sometimes, abuse situations are not labeled until one is triggered much later in life. An example provided to me in a grad class: when the victim has a daughter, who turns the age at which the mother was abused. Should not the questions for present to ask oneself as a helper include: How is she identifying affects, or has she? How can it not control today if not identified and the effect controlled? Be careful here... if I am in a position for something abusive to be controlling me at this moment, then I am certainly in need of standing with the armor God gives for the fight. Consequently, I firmly state that the <u>current</u> affects be addressed by the negativity being produced in the present identified. Probably producing some unexpected goals for the present day. Obviously in the example from that college class...a present-tense child is involved in this one! I will fight someone stating that scenario should be forgotten...too much negativity there that may affect the innocent, agreed?

One must be at a place strong enough to gain or to re-gain required control. The abuse may never be forgotten any more than the triggers disappearing for life. A person with an abusive story experiences triggers just as others do. Should I preach or label you as wrong to be thinking of a loved one on the anniversary of his/her death each year spoiling an otherwise lovely day? Or would it be better to have a discussion as to the best way to handle that trigger each year the date comes around? After all, triggers are not required to be negative; some may be used as a cause for celebration. If the trigger still affects you today, then, somehow it may be included by you as a significant part of your life story. I cannot imagine spending my time today doing what I am doing without having experienced my life-story. Maybe He sometimes has us experience the negativity to 'get it'; in addition to use it as a great help for another...consequently, the negative becomes a positive because we have something to offer the broken one which may be helpful.

I believe the scenarios in our life story play a descriptive role in the reasons we are who we are today. And I think God knows everything in each chapter of my entire story. I can identify life scenarios which made me uneasy, or happy--warm fuzzies, as well as uncomfortable settings; I assume you can easily do the same. If we were sitting together today and a tree fell across in front of us, we would likely explain it differently...no right/no wrong/ but different. I believe my life story is an important piece that defines me today as yours does you. Please do not require me to put on a facade and pretend it is non-existent because it is uncomfortable. You are not required to ask me what the screaming was in the pet-scan room. If you choose to ask me, however, I believe I have the right not be required to 'make up' an answer. Hopefully, you have not already shown me that I am not equal/OK/capable of making my own choices by identifying for me what you believe I should have chosen to do in that or another circumstance without my having asked your opinion.

I am surely glad God does not assign me to save another; and that what He does assign me I will be able to do, hopefully because I have prayed a lot and paid close attention to His guidance. I am thankful that God is helping me learn to use the strength He gifts to be honest and open with the church family. I am excited that I am recognizing church leadership willing to help me with scripture and questions I have as well as preparing sermons and patiently accepting interruptions in classes with my questions enabling me to, hopefully, help others with credibility.

This thought occurred to me while walking the dog the other day: Maybe it will be good to include here for all believers who desire to help others keep in mind: When He walked on earth with other humans, Jesus stood and faced the devil when being tempted on earth stating the Word of God in the Bible. He also made certain this information was there for me to learn: When hanging on the cross covered in <u>my</u> sin, Jesus questioned God: *"...My God, my God, why have you forsaken me?"* (NIV Mark 15:34 p1106) This verse tells me that, being a man on this earth who was covered in <u>my</u> sin, Jesus gets me...even when I am broken. I have tried to find the words to express how over-the-top powerful this message is to me and I cannot. But I understand clearly that if people are right to say, "You've got to experience abuse to 'get it'"...Well, HE certainly did that and He did it by choice for us! I have recently shared that thought with others and the reactions encouraged me to never forget how powerful this message is for an abuse victim. If a believer is in the 'victim' place and self-defining as broken, unable to feel God's presence, or love, or understanding, or patience; I not only identify that they are frustrated by that; but that it also is affecting their self-description. If I am yelling at HIM that I cannot feel Him, He's not there...blah blah blah. .... He not only understands but He relates to it. HE'S BEEN THERE!!! He is with me...patiently waiting rather than judging. This is what I have shared with friends and will readily share with others I assume are believers who are broken and crying when talking to me. I think it helps the 'victim' use that strength and energy elsewhere. I know, when I start struggling, it helps me to <u>not</u> lose the sense of HIS presence; but rather to just talk to Him. The third message that God has pointed out to me very recently and helpful for my self-concept issue involves the man in the Bible that wrote more Books within God's Word than anyone else. You know... that one who met with world leaders... that one who was known to all so readily that other men were referred to as being with Paul. The day I was in that Bible class and they were discussing the tent-making process and how 'yucky' it was...'stinky'...I was shocked by my excitement. I knew Paul made tents if he needed money, but I did not know that God assigned him a job that would cause me to turn and walk on the other side of the field! (This helps me now when someone turns and walks away from me when I have shared a past story of my life.) I now can accept that Jesus sees me as an equal (not saying I do not have a problem sometimes reflecting that belief). I can readily accept the fact that He has a job for even me. It is easier today to accept than it has ever been for me before. He Gave me the necessities to face the devil including the same weapon He used (and it is concrete!). He is sitting in Heaven right now with scars that have my name. And He put Paul, of all the people in the Bible, in a job which was more physically tiring and stinky than the job I had walking home from High School to clean a man's apartment and toilet. I think the next time another turns and walks away from me after I have shared a story of my past as they just have also; I will not tell Jesus that He's picked the wrong one for my job. And Jesus has also allowed me to experience how helpful it is to people like me.

I cannot help but wonder if, just perhaps, that may be one reason why Christ came to earth for you and me, as well as any other who chooses Him. I have Support right here next to me as I am typing this very moment. Support coming from one Who definitely 'gets me'.... One who suffered much worse than I .... One Who chose to take my place and suffer to the extreme that He asked the question while on the cross…. One Whose love is for me cost Him the 'concrete' scars with my name on them lasting for eternity …. He understands me better than I or the human with whom I am sharing. So, I will identify Him as the top One to go to for help and guidance when I am the one struggling <u>or </u>the one who is trying to help another.

THANK YOU, JESUS !

Printed in the United States
by Baker & Taylor Publisher Services